D1537801

War and Rank Among Nations

War and Rank Among Nations

Michael David Wallace

Lexington Books
D.C. Heath and Company
Lexington, Massachusetts
Toronto   London

327.072
W155w

C. L. HARDY LIBRARY
ATLANTIC CHRISTIAN COLLEGE
WILSON, N. C. 27893

Library of Congress Cataloging in Publication Data

Wallace, Michael David.
  War and rank among nations.

  Bibliography: p.
  1. International relations—Research. 2. War. I. Title.
JX1291.W35   327'.07'2   73-1137
ISBN 0-669-85191-4

Copyright © 1973 by D.C. Heath and Company.

All rights reserved. No part of this publication may be reproduced or transmitted in any form or by any means, electronic or mechanical, including photocopy, recording, or any information storage or retrieval system, without permission in writing from the publisher.

Published simultaneously in Canada.

Printed in the United States of America.

International Standard Book Number: 0-669-85191-4

Library of Congress Catalog Card Number: 73-1137

Contents

75- 638

List of Tables

Preface

It is a pleasure to record the many debts incurred in the writing of this book. The Canada Council provided support for the author in the first stages of the research. The University of British Columbia furnished computer time and facilities, and their Statistical Center provided guidance with the programming and statistics. My wife, Eileen, helped edit and type the first draft; Ms. Michelle Marcouiller prepared the final typescript.

The most heartfelt acknowledgment is due the Correlates of War Project at the University of Michigan, and particularly its director, Professor J. David Singer. Not only did this enterprise generate most of the data used here, but it also provided a firm theoretical and methodological base from which the present effort could be launched. I am also deeply indebted to Professor Singer both for the many hours he freely gave to the discussion of the ideas presented here, and for his many insightful suggestions concerning the manuscript.

War and Rank Among Nations

1 Inequality and Violence

In the natural course of human affairs it must necessarily happen, that some of mankind will live in plenty and opulence, and others be reduced to a state of indigence and poverty. The former need the labors of the latter, and the latter the provision and support of the former. This mutual necessity is the foundation of that connection, whether we call it moral or civil, which subsists between masters and servants (Encyclopaedia Britannica, 1771, p. 290).

The Japanese insist that their military action in Korea and in Manchuria and northern China has also been similar to the military action of the United States in the Caribbean. They maintain that they have merely been applying the "police power doctrine" of President Theodore Roosevelt. They claim that in overthrowing the Chinese Government in Manchuria, Japan was abating a neighborhood nuisance, as the United States did when it overthrew the Spanish Government in Cuba; that in recognizing the independence of Manchukuo, they were following the example of the United States in its recognition of Panama; and that their entire course of action in Manchuria has been in line with the American policy in the Caribbean region as manifested by American military interventions in Mexico, Nicaragua, Haiti and the Dominican Republic.

Although there are certain similarities between the respective positions, policies and actions of the United States and Japan there are also decided differences. The position of Japan in Asia in certain important respects fails to parallel that of the United States in America. The United States is a vast territory with a great population vis-à-vis a dozen Caribbean republics, each with a relatively small area and population. Japan, on the other hand, is a country with a relatively small area and population vis-à-vis the vast territory and great population of China. An attitude which therefore appears natural for the United States to take toward the Caribbean states does not appear natural for Japan to take toward China (Blakeslee, 1933, pp. 677-8).

Introduction

In the eighth decade of the twentieth century, few can be found who are willing to quarrel with the principle of the legal equality of all men and women in human society. It is the cornerstone of political legitimacy in most states, and politicians continually cleave to it, at least verbally. So powerful has been its attraction that those nations whose political systems retain any substantial degree of formal inequality (such as South Africa) find themselves pariahs in the international community.

Yet we are all too well aware that the triumph of equality has been far less noticeable in the actual conduct of social affairs than in the solemn pronouncements of officialdom. Not only does social inequality in its various guises provide a major animus for contemporary politics, but the concepts referring to inequality—class, status, stratification, position, hierarchy, elite, and power—are still fundamental to the analysis of virtually every aspect of human social existence. Even when not employed overtly as variables in analysis, they are used to delimit the universe of research itself, as in studies of "lower-class adolescents."

Nowhere have these concepts played a more crucial role than in the explanation of social conflict. For over a century the main thrust of theoretical and empirical scholarship has emphasized the fundamental role of social stratification broadly conceived in generating the tensions, disputes, and violence existing in society. This emphasis has, of course, received its primary impetus from Marxist theory, but many non-Marxists—de Toqueville, Beard, Durkheim, and Weber among them—have all posited a connection between social hierarchy and violence, without necessarily agreeing with the Marxists about which sort of hierarchy generates conflict or the dynamic by which it does so. Building on this very extensive speculative literature, there has grown up a large body of empirical findings linking status and hierarchy to social conflict.

Given the crucial role played by status variables in the explanation of *domestic* conflict, one might expect that hierarchy and status within the international system would constitute important elements in any explanation of international war. Of course, simplified parallels between international and domestic systems can be dangerously misleading. But given the overt strife generated by status differences even in well-regulated societies, it certainly would seem worthwhile to examine the relationship between status and violence in the far more anarchic milieu of the international system.

The purpose of this book will be to explore some aspects of this relationship, in the hope that status will prove as powerful an explanatory variable in the search for the causes of war between nations as it has come to be in the study of domestic violence and revolution. In particular, this study will attempt to draw upon some segments of the copious literature linking status and conflict within societies in order to obtain insights and hypotheses which may help explain violence between nations. These hypotheses will then be tested by adducing data from the international system.

Status in the International System

Now it may be objected at the outset that the very anarchy of the international system renders meaningless any concept of hierarchy or stratification. The notion of status ordering in a social system implies far more than a mere continuum of deference and reward. First, hierarchy usually implies a differentiation of social tasks; as the quotation at the beginning of this chapter implies, different positions on the hierarchy entail different social functions. A second concomitant is inevitably a set of procedures for determining placement on the hierarchy, and some mechanism to enforce this placement. While criteria for determining status position may be crude indeed in some societies, they always involve the application of regularized procedures except under conditions of social disintegration. Although some have argued that many aspects of social structure at the international level resemble primitive human societies (Masters, 1964), the consensus of international relations scholars seems to be that functional differentiation is scarcely observable in the international system (Hoffmann, 1960, p. 47) and it is obvious that national behavior is constrained very little by commonly accepted rules. International society resembles less an organized community than Hobbes' state of nature, a war of all against all in which benefits and rewards are distributed almost entirely according to the doctrine of self-help. There is little reason, then, to take for granted the relevance and utility of concepts such as status and hierarchy which were developed to describe features of much more highly differentiated and regulated social systems.

Nevertheless, there is no lack of evidence that something resembling a hierarchy does indeed exist in the international system. Reference to the existence of a "pecking order" is a commonplace in the traditional literature of international relations and in the folklore of diplomacy. While the more formalized trappings of international hierarchy embodied in such institutions as the Holy Roman Empire have long since fallen before the onslaught of "sovereign equality," the widespread use of such terms as "superpower," "major power," or—less flatteringly—"banana republic" should serve to remind us that the society of nations is by no means a classless one. To be sure, the norms of courtesy among allies and friends dictate that major powers shall often defer to smaller nations on minor matters. Yet hierarchy reasserts itself dramatically in times of crisis, whether the issue be the outbreak of armed conflict or a run on gold. At such crucial times, it is the understood privilege and duty of the "influentials" to initiate remedial measures and play the predominant role in their execution. Only when the major nations fail are "middle powers" cast in the role of peacemakers (Claude, 1963).

International organizations often formally embody this hierarchy in their constitutions. The major nations are assessed a larger share of the organizational expenditures and in return are entitled to a correspondingly greater voice in the affairs of the organization. These or analogous procedures have been adopted by organizations ranging from the Universal Postal Union to the Common Market to the World Bank. Even so self-consciously egalitarian a body as the United Nations, which does not tie voting strength to contributions, makes a formal constitutional distinction between ordinary state members and the privileged few who are permanent members of the Security Council.

Thus, there would appear to be some sort of status ordering in the international system despite the lack of a really cohesive social structure. The reason, of course, lies in the widely differing innate capabilities of the various national actors. In the contemporary international system, nations vary in the size of their populations by almost four orders of magnitude, with even larger discrepancies existing in area, gross national product, natural resources, and military capability (Russett et al., 1958). The extreme inequalities of the present period did not always characterize the international system (Lagos, 1963, pp. 10-12) but at no time in modern history has the situation resembled the approximate equality of innate capability which characterizes the actors in domestic society. In the latter,

nature hath made men so equal . . . as that though there be found one man sometimes manifestly stronger in body or quicker in mind . . . it is not so considerable, as that one man can thereupon claim to himself any benefit (Hobbes, 1955, p. 80).

But, in international society, differences in capability have been sufficiently great to produce a hierarchy of reward and deference amongst the nations of the international system.

In short, while the concepts of hierarchy and status may indeed be usefully applied in the international context, they must undergo some transformation in the process. The international hierarchy would seem more analogous to the pecking order amongst chickens in a barnyard than the status relationships between individuals and groups in human societies. Consequently, in adapting hypotheses from sociology or social psychology to the international arena one must take into account the "slippage" between the two contexts. Given the volume of social science literature dealing with the status-conflict relationship, it would seem best to begin by examining how this relationship has been conceived in the existing theoretical and empirical literature of international relations, turning to the other social sciences once it has been discovered where they may be of most assistance.

Power and Status

As was noted above, hierarchy in the international system is based very largely on differences in size and capability among nations. It is therefore not surprising that international relations scholars who have treated the subject of status and hierarchy have done so almost exclusively in terms of the concept of power. This equation of power and hierarchy is most clearly expressed by Deutsch (1968, p. 22):

Power, most simply and crudely put, is the ability to prevail in conflict. . . . Who will get his way and who will have to give in? Such questions as these, when asked about many possible encounters among a limited number of competitors, lead to rank lists—such as the rankings of players in tennis or chess tournaments, of baseball clubs in the world series, of chickens in the peck order of a chicken yard, and of great powers in world politics.[1]

While this concept of a power hierarchy is useful for some analytic purposes (Organski, 1968) it is deficient in one crucial respect; it portrays hierarchy in the international system as a single, univocal ranking or status ordering. At best, this is a considerable oversimplification.

First, this ranking will vary from one area to another. As Boulding (1962) has pointed out, nations have "power gradients" even in the atomic age. Not even the strongest nations are able to influence events in all areas with equal ease. The obvious example is the strikingly different hierarchy prevailing in Eastern Europe and the North Atlantic area. Despite the predominance of the super-powers within their own orbits, events have demonstrated that they have little direct influence on the other side of the ideological line.

Second, the status position of nations is not the same for all issue areas. Some nations, of course, have a very broad spectrum of influence, but this is not always the case. For example, while the voice of the U.S.S.R. is critically important in global military matters, it is marginal with regard to most economic questions; the reader is invited to compare its role in the Geneva disarmament negotiations with that in the 1968 UNCTAD conference. The opposite situation pertains with regard to Japan, whose economic influence is felt throughout the world although it does not formally even have armed forces.

Third, there is not always a correspondence between the major material components of capability and the actual ability to influence outcomes (Singer, 1963). Very large nations, or ones with rapidly expanding industrial and military capabilities, may not always be able to obtain influence proportional to their resources; until recently, China was an outstanding example. Conversely, nations in strategic locations or those which for other reasons are crucial to the interests of larger nations, can often obtain a degree of deference and influence quite out of keeping with their material capacities (Morgenthau, 1968, pp. 106-8).

Lastly, there are many facets of status and deference between nations which can scarcely be subsumed under the rubric of power (Galtung, 1964, pp. 116-8). Historical traditions, cultural and other achievements of individuals within a nation, and the general attractiveness of a nation's life style and social and political organization generate many positive and negative evaluations which can constitute an important aspect of national status. On these dimensions, nations such as Sweden or Switzerland score relatively high, while pariahs such as South Africa and Haiti are near the bottom. At least in these extreme cases, it is not difficult to demonstrate the effect of such collective evaluations on the status hierarchy of the international system.

In short, just as Weber (1953) found a unidimensional concept of hierarchy predicated solely on economic relations within a society to be of limited explanatory utility, so must we regard a unidimensional concept of hierarchy based on power in the international system. It is more useful to conceive of a nation as having positions on a wide variety of rank dimensions, or, to use the sociological terminology, as having a status set rather than a single status. Returning to our basic concern, we may now ask: what is the relationship between this multidimensional status ordering and the genesis of international violence? Since social scientists have concentrated a good deal of effort studying multidimensional status hierarchies within domestic societies, it would seem appropriate at this juncture to turn to an examination of some of their hypotheses and findings. It turns out, indeed, that an examination of the social science literature on multidimensional hierarchies suggests many parallels with the international system.

Status Inconsistency and Sociological Theory

Implicit in the multidimensional approach to the study of social stratification is the assumption that an individual's rankings on different status dimensions will sometimes diverge. For example, if "socio-economic status" is no longer conceptualized as a single variable, but broken down into prestige and economic dimensions, then an individual or group may rank high on one and low on the other. Of course, it is likely that in most societies the major dimensions of social hierarchy will be highly correlated, and therefore that the number of individuals with substantial inconsistencies in their status set will usually be quite low (Hyman, 1966; Lenski, 1966, p. 88). Nonetheless, because social status is such an important predictor of attitudes and behavior, some scholars have become interested in the possible impact of such inconsistent statuses on an individual or a group.

Many hold the opinion that such inconsistencies exert profoundly disturbing effects on a society. According to this view, the greatest social tensions do not necessarily arise from the existence of hierarchies and the consequent unequal distribution of social value *per se*. While there is no doubt an ever-present tendency for the "underdogs" of society to revolt against their lot, challenging the power and privilege of the "topdogs," there are many instances—ancient and contemporary—of highly stratified and unequal societies avoiding or successfully repressing dissension and revolt for centuries at a time (Lenski, 1966, Chapters 8-9). This is explained at least in part by the fact that the underdogs have been well socialized into their role; while they receive little, they have never come to expect more than they have. If we grant that this process of "inequality socialization" is not always adequate in depth or scope, we would expect maximum social tension to occur when deprivation is combined with the expectation of reward, and indeed there appears to be solid empirical evidence that this is so (Cofer & Appley, 1964). The question then becomes, under what circumstances are high expectations combined with deprivation relative to these expectations? The answer given by many sociologists would be, when an individual's rankings on two or more dimensions of social hierarchy are markedly inconsistent (Lenski, 1966, pp. 86-90; Galtung, 1964). In social interactions which emphasize the higher of his statuses, he will receive the deference and rewards of (relatively) high position, and this will form the basis of his expectations. When these rewards are not forthcoming in social inter-actions which stress his lower status, he perceives this as deprivation and feels himself treated inequitably:

One can see how this works, and the consequences of it, by imagining the interaction of a Negro doctor and a white laborer in a situation where neither the racial nor occupational status system alone is relevant. The former, motivated by self-interest, will strive to establish the relation on the basis of occupation (or perhaps education or wealth), while the latter, similarly moti-vated, will strive to establish the relationship on the basis of race. Since each regards his own point of view as right and proper, and since neither is likely to view the problem in a detached, analytical fashion, one or both are likely to be frustrated, and probably angered, by the experience (Lenski, 1966, p. 87).

Of course, all such inconsistencies will not produce tensions. If the dis-crepancy in rankings has become institutionalized by one means or another, it will not be a source of frustration (Wesolowski, 1966). An example of such institutionalized discrepancy might be that of the clergyman whose high social standing is seldom matched by financial remuneration. Moreover, feelings of deprivation or frustration experienced by status inconsistent individuals need not and often will not be expressed as hostility to the social order if there exist socially approved channels for upward mobility on their low-status dimension. But, "where legal, customary, or other barriers seriously hamper the equilibrat-ing tendency, social tensions of revolutionary magnitude may be generated" (Benoit-Smullyan, 1944).

A good deal of empirical evidence has been put forward in support of this theory. In a study of college sophomores, Fenchel et al. (1951) discovered that an individual whose statuses were inconsistent from one reference group to another exhibited a significantly greater amount of "status striving." Adams (1963) found that bomber crews whose members had inconsistent rankings on dimensions salient to military personnel (rank, length of service, age, and education) functioned less harmoniously than status consistent crews. In separate studies, Clark (1958), Sayles (1958), and Adams (1963a) reported both disharmony and reduced productivity in work relations when there was a perceived inconsistency between a worker's job status and his qualifications as measured by age, education, and experience. Lenski (1956), working with data derived from the Detroit Area Survey, produced complementary findings:

individuals whose ethnic, income, occupational, and educational statuses were not consistent, joined fewer voluntary organizations, participated less actively in the ones they did join, and reported less often that their participation was motivated by a desire for pleasurable social contact. Jackson (1962) reported that such individuals also exhibited a greater degree of psychological stress and, in some cases, greater personal aggressiveness.

In addition to these effects on personal attitudes and behavior, status inconsistency has been found to have an important influence on political attitudes and behavior. Lenski (1954) found that status inconsistent individuals were more likely to vote Democrat and to hold liberal political views. Lipset (1959) found that high status individuals belonging to a minority religion (Protestants in Catholic countries or Catholics in Protestant countries) were more likely to belong to left-of-center parties. Goffmann (1957) reported that status inconsistents were more likely to favor extensive changes in the existing pattern of power relationships in society. Finally, in an examination of twenty-five national surveys of voting behavior in Australia, Britain, Canada, and the United States, Lenski (1967) found a very strong association between status inconsistency and tendency to vote for left of center parties.

Even more directly relevant to the present concern is a study of rioters in the Detroit and Newark ghettos by Caplan and Paige (1968). Although they did not use the phrase, it would appear that their "typical rioter" was a status inconsistent individual—a person above his peers in education and acquired skills, but unable to obtain employment or remuneration commensurate with these attributes. Still other studies suggest that another status inconsistent group common in the Third World—the educated unemployed—are a major source of political opposition in most developing nations and often are an important destabilizing social force (Galtung, 1964; Shils, 1960).

Status Inconsistency and Conflict—Some Objections

Despite this evidence, a number of objections can be raised with regard to status inconsistency models of conflict. First, it could be argued that since the number of status inconsistent individuals is inevitably rather small, they cannot be responsible for any great amount of social conflict. But Lenski points out that the very inconsistent position which leads them to challenge the existing status distribution also provides them with power weapons to do so:

The great majority of the supporters of liberal and radical movements will probably always be persons of consistently low status. Such movements also require *leaders* and *resources*, however, and persons of consistently low status are not likely to have either the training or the skills necessary to lead such movements successfully, nor are they likely to have money to spare. By contrast, persons of inconsistent status are frequently in a position to supply one or both of these necessary ingredients thus greatly increasing the probability of the success of such movements. As a result, their importance may well be out of all proportion to their numbers (Lenski, 1966, p. 88).

A more important objection is that the status inconsistency theory appears at least in partial disagreement with another major body of theory and evidence in the social science literature, variously known as the "crosscut" or "cross-pressure" theory. Scholars who adopt this approach suggest that inconsistencies in an individual's social position or group affiliation may actually lead to the control and moderation of social conflict. In contrast to the previous theory, it is assumed that a complete polarization between "topdogs" and "underdogs" can of itself lead to a breakdown of social order (Coser, 1956, pp. 76-7; Galtung, 1966). It is argued that each dimension of social division—color, caste, wealth, occupation, lineage or whatever—contains within it a potential conflict whenever the disparate groups encounter one another. For example, America experiences conflicts between black and white, rich and poor, blue collar and professional, because color, wealth, and job prestige are central to the determination of an individual's standing in the community. Given these cleavages, what is at issue is not the presence or absence of conflict but its intensity.

Now if all dimensions of social hierarchy were perfectly correlated so that there were no inconsistencies (e.g., if all blacks were poor and unskilled), the net effect would be to increase the intensity of conflict, since divisions along each dimension of hierarchy would tend to reinforce one another, polarizing the society into "haves" and "have nots." Such a single intense conflict might, according to some, be sufficient to destroy the society itself.

It has been persuasively argued that inconsistencies in the status ordering prevent this polarization by ensuring that different dimensions of social value will split the society in different ways; those who are "underdogs" on one issue may be "topdogs" on the next, and vice versa. E.A. Ross (1920, pp. 164-5) has expressed the general line of argument in an apt metaphor:

These different oppositions in a society are like different wave series set upon opposite sides of a lake, which neutralize each other if the crest of one meets the trough of the other. . . . A society, therefore, which is ridden by a dozen oppositions along lines running in every direction may actually be in less danger of being torn with violence or falling to pieces than one split along just one line. For each new cleavage contributes to narrow the cross clefts, so that one might say that society is *sewn together* by its inner conflicts.

This line of argument cannot be dismissed as mere speculation. In their classic study, Berelson, Lazarsfeld and McPhee (1954) did discover that "cross-pressured" individuals were much less predictable in their behavior when faced with a stimulus requiring an unambiguous "low status" or "high status" response. For example, Catholic or Jewish professionals are less reliable in their choice of the

Republican party than their Protestant colleagues. Another study (Campbell et al., 1960) showed that inconsistency between occupational and subjective status apparently produces the same result; such individuals are less reliable in their party affiliation and less involved politically.

Moreover, there is some evidence to suggest that such status inconsistent individuals have a greater degree of political tolerance towards opposing political groups and opinions (Lipset, 1959). Additional (albeit less operational) corroberation is to be found in case studies of national political systems. One well-known study is Weiner's analysis (1962) of group pressures in Indian politics. He argues that the multiplicity of crosscutting status pressures actually tends to facilitate the management of conflict; when competing pressures are polarized, political stability is endangered.

However, despite its persuasiveness the "crosscutting" model stops well short of posing a serious obstacle to the status inconsistency explanation of conflict, for two reasons. First, the two theories are by no means mutually incompatible.[2] For one thing, many of the "cleavages" spoken of by the cross-pressure theory are not in fact rank dimensions at all. The division of a bureaucracy into specialized departments referred to by Coser (1956) is one example; in some societies, the same may be true of religion, language, and ethnicity. Here the separation is less vertical than horizontal; "crosscutting group membership" in such situations does not necessarily imply status inconsistency. It is also noteworthy that both hypotheses consider status discrepancies to be disturbing stimuli to the people concerned; they differ only with respect to the reactions attributed to these individuals. Cross-pressure theorists hypothesize the response to be one of passivity and withdrawal; the inconsistency interpretation posits aggression as the more probable response. Suggestive studies by Kenkel (1956) and Jackson (1962) offer some evidence that these differing reactions may be produced by differing sorts of status inconsistency.

For one thing, the effects of status inconsistency appear to be very specific to certain combinations of rank-dimensions which Jackson labels "achieved" and "ascribed"; the most significant effects are produced when the inconsistency is between a dimension on which mobility is possible (education, income, or occupational prestige) and one in which it is not (such as race or ethnicity). It also matters which of the two statuses is the lower. If an "ascribed" status is lower, the individual's response is likely to be extrapunitive or aggressive; if his "achieved" status is lower the response will be intrapunitive, often resulting in withdrawal.

Segal (1968) adduces further evidence that the contradiction between these two hypotheses is more apparent than real. He finds that status inconsistency leads to support for social change when a person's lower status is socially visible, and thus creates a gap between self-assessed status and that assigned by others. This applies in the case of racial minorities who have achieved middle class income levels. On the other hand, when a person's contradictory statuses are not visible but are salient only to his personal political choice, the most likely response is withdrawal. The large number of upper and middle income Catholics who refused to indicate party preference in the 1960 presidential campaign appears to confirm this.

Even to the extent that the two approaches are directly in opposition, this need not necessarily represent a formidable objection to the status inconsistency theory. Much of the cross-pressure evidence is nonoperational in character, especially case studies such as Weiner's. For one thing, what level of conflict is being used as a baseline? By comparison with some other Asian societies, India has been relatively peaceful; yet, compared with many other institutional democracies (many of which do not manifest a crosscutting social structure) India's political system exhibits an intolerable amount of violence. It is difficult to see how, on the basis of such evidence, we are to determine the real influence of the cross-pressure effect. Furthermore, case studies of other nations fail to yield the same results; Eckstein (1966) asserts that in Norway the laying of new social divisions across the old has exacerbated social conflict.

It would seem there is little in the cross-pressure model to detract seriously from either the evidential base or the intuitive plausibility of the status inconsistency theory of conflict. To be sure, it is still too early to state categorically that "the hypothesis has been well confirmed" (1964, p. 104). Most tests have been limited both with regard to methodology and domain, (Hyman, 1966) and in some cases contradictory evidence has been discovered (Kenkel, 1950; Kelly and Chambliss, 1966). Nevertheless, this model would appear to be a good point of departure for any examination of the relationship between multidimensional hierarchy in the international system and the onset of international violence. Is there a status inconsistency effect in the international context analogous to the one observed within societies? Before this question can be answered, it is first necessary to establish that a plausible analogy with respect to this hypothesis exists between domestic and international systems, and then to spell out in what form international status inconsistency may be expected to lead to violent conflict between nations. The next chapter is devoted to this task.

Notes

1. Karl W. Deutsch, THE ANALYSIS OF INTERNATIONAL RELATIONS © 1968. Reprinted by permission of Prentice-Hall, Inc., Englewood Cliffs, New Jersey.

2. A detailed discussion of some of the ambiguities in the various versions of the cross-pressure model is contained in Rae and Taylor (1970).

2

Status Inconsistency in the International System

Introduction

As noted in the previous chapter, transferring a theory of individual behavior to the international system as an hypothesis about the behavior of nation-states inevitably produces some conceptual "slippage." We may identify three aspects of the sociologists' status inconsistency model which require careful examination and some modification if continuity of meaning is to be preserved. These are: a) the specific dimensions of stratification to be examined, b) the mechanisms through which inconsistencies are alleged to lead to increased aggression and conflict, and c) the allowance made for the possible contaminating effects of other status variables.

The Dimensions of Hierarchy

Dubious Analogies (I)—Domestic Status Dimensions

The sociological literature presents us with many rich and suggestive taxonomies of the status dimensions important in various domestic social systems as well as many different ways of producing operational indices of the various sorts of status and hierarchy (Lenski, 1966). While it is tempting to draw upon these established usages in the construction of hypotheses about status at the international level, it is doubtful that they will meet our needs, for three reasons.

First, many important status dimensions at the domestic level do not have any obvious counterparts at the international level, since they involve aspects of social control and differentiation which do not exist or are poorly developed in the international system. For example, in the absence of significant functional differentiation amongst national actors it is difficult to conceive of an international equivalent to occupational prestige.

Second, even if we grant that some dimensions of domestic hierarchy have approximate international analogs, these certainly stop well short of being isomorphic. To take an obvious example, both nations and individuals may be ranked on various dimensions of wealth or economic well-being. But while the personal wealth of an individual in society always depends on exchanges with others, the wealth of a nation is only partly a function of outside interaction; it is primarily a function of a complex set of processes internal to the actor itself.

13

There is every likelihood, therefore, that economic status in these two contexts would affect behavior in quite different ways.

Finally, the *importance* of a particular dimension is often altered markedly when we shift to its analog at the international level. On the one hand, except in conditions of civil turmoil, military capability is scarcely significant as a group or individual attribute within a domestic society, but is obviously a crucial attribute of nations in the international system. On the other hand, race, religion and culture are clearly less important as status characteristics between nations than within them; even the most firmly held status evaluations based on such factors may be upset by other dimensions of evaluation, as witnessed by the granting of *de jure* "white" status to the Japanese by such racist regimes as Nazi Germany and contemporary South Africa.

Dubious Analogies (II)–Achieved and Ascribed Status

Given these difficulties in selecting specific rank-dimensions paralleling those in domestic social systems, most investigations of status inconsistency amongst nations (East, 1969; Fossum, 1967; Midlarsky, 1969) have attempted to construe the analogy less directly by extending the sociological distinction between "achieved" and "ascribed" status into the international system. Just as individuals are considered to have some status rankings which primarily reflect personal achievement (education, skills) and some which are inalterably imposed by the structure and culture of the system (race, ethnicity), so it is argued that a nation's status set contains both rankings over which it has a large measure of control (military capability, economic development) and those which are largely determined by the collective action of the comity of nations, such as prestige and recognition. Since Jackson (1962) and others have discovered that the greatest inconsistency effect in the domestic context appears to occur when the discrepancy is between an achieved and an ascribed status, scholars studying inconsistency at the international level have focused upon what they conceive to be discrepancies between achieved and ascribed status in the international context.

But however satisfactory such a taxonomy may be in sociology, its applicability to the international system is open to grave doubt; the concepts of achieved and ascribed status contain important ambiguities when used to refer to national rank position. Unfortunately, these ambiguities are reflected in many of the studies examining the effects of status inconsistency in the international system.

The reader may recall that ascribed status as used above referred to those aspects of social position which cannot be altered. Note, however, that their permanency presupposes two conditions: (a) that the characteristic on which the evaluation is based (being black, of royal blood, or a harijan) cannot be changed, and (b) that the social evaluation of this characteristic is fixed by the structure and culture of the society. If either ceases to hold, mobility is possible; when individuals "pass" or black becomes beautiful, race will no longer automatically place a person.

Now it should be evident that nations do not possess "ascribed status" in any sense which meets the two conditions set forth above. It is quite useful to conceive of an international consensus or collective judgment as producing a status ordering of nations, (Singer and Small, 1966) but nations can and do attain considerable mobility in this hierarchy by war, economic expansion, or social and economic development. Such a status position is "ascribed" in the sense that it is imposed from without by others in the social system, but this does not carry the connotations of fixity and caste that are concomitant with the sociological usage; it has more in common with occupational prestige (an "achieved" status in sociological parlance) than with race or ethnicity.

If it is misleading to refer to attributed importance as "ascribed" status solely because it is based on evaluations external to the nation, it is doubly confusing when the label is attached to characteristics which, while usually fixed and immutable, are not usually considered as status characteristics. For example, short of a war of territorial aggrandizement, a nation's geographical area is "ascribed" in the sense of being fixed (Fossum, 1967), but it is obvious that nations seldom attribute status to each other on the basis of area in the same manner or degree that individuals attribute status on the basis of skin color.

It would seem, then, that studies of status inconsistency at the international level have used the notion of "ascribed status" to refer to two quite different types of characteristics, neither of which is isomorphic with its sociological usage. The concept of "achieved status" fares little better. The difficulty in applying it to the international system centers around the fact that nations, unlike individuals, are not irreducible entities, but social coalitions whose separate and several members possess their own perceptions, goals, and values. While we may speak metaphorically of a nation as an actor in an international social system, it will not do to forget that national "achievement" is measured not only in terms of a nation's success in obtaining power, privilege, and prestige within that system, but also by its success in satisfying and maximizing the material and nonmaterial values and goals of its constituent members. In other words, a nation may be evaluated either as an actor jostling for advantage in the international system or as a society "delivering the goods" to its citizens.

It is hardly likely that these two forms of "achieved status" will always coincide, as was intimated in the discussion of rank dimensions in Chapter 1. Status as an *international actor* will be characterized by high scores on indices which reflect the absolute magnitude of national resources; gross national product, size of national budget, defense expenditure, and industrial production are examples. Status as a *society*, on the other hand, is conceived of as the way resources are made available to the populace; G.N.P. per capita, health, welfare, and educational spending and equality of income distribution are useful indices here. Despite the divergence between these two rank-dimensions, both are termed "achieved status" in much of the literature (Midlarsky, 1969; East, 1969; Galtung, 1966). Once again it would appear that the sociological term is misplaced in the international context.

All in all, then it seems difficult to justify selecting and labelling rank-dimensions at the international level by analogy from the domestic social system. This does not mean, however, that they must be chosen arbitrarily; upon closer examination, the status inconsistency model itself provides some measure of guidance, as shall now be demonstrated.

Capability and Inconsistency

In the previous chapter evidence was presented which linked the disturbing impact of status inconsistency to the individual's tendency to tie all his status expectations to his high standing on one or two dimensions. When these expectations are disappointed with regard to some *other* important dimension, the individual experiences tension and frustration. Thus, to select those status discrepancies which are likely to be important at the *international* level, we must first determine which rank-dimension or dimensions forms the basis for *national*[1] status expectations.

While many different attributes may play this role for individuals (Lenski, 1954), it is clearly capability which determines national status expectations. As detailed in the previous chapter, the lack of "artificial impediments" to goal attainment in the international system means that capability will be the most crucial factor in determining position in the international hierarchy. While it is of course by no means the *only* relevant status factor in international interaction, national actors have in general expected rewards, deference, satisfactions, and benefits to be divided in a way that effects their capability ranking. If this situation does not obtain in some critical area over a period of time, it would seem likely that a sense of grievance and injustice will develop amongst those national decision-makers whose nation's capabilities are not matched by suitable status rewards (Galtung, 1964, pp. 98-100).

It is not too difficult to conceive of conflict resulting from such grievances when they are permitted to accumulate. With status inconsistency providing the motive, a relatively high level of capability the means, and the lack of effective restraints in the international system the opportunity, it is more than likely some nations may respond with aggressive or warlike actions (Galtung, 1964, p. 101).

The only remaining question, then is what are the *other* status dimensions that are part of this equation? If expectations are fixed by reference to capability, what dimensions of the international pecking order are the target of these aspirations?

Reputational Status

Although nations seem to define their status expectations fairly unambiguously in terms of their capabilities, the other forms of status sought by nations are neither so easily identifiable nor so constant over space and time. The number and heterogeneity of these rankings are legion: security, influence, prestige, colonies, and relative economic advantage are amongst the attributes most often cited. Far less attention has been paid to these aspects of national status than to capability, and outside of the work of Singer and Small (1966) no operational indicators have been developed to measure them which are suitable for comparisons over any extended period of time.

As a consequence of the lack of careful conceptual and empirical specification in this area, the use of such rank-dimensions in this study poses grave problems. For one thing, some forms of status vary widely in importance over space and time, and thus are not suitable for inclusion in a study which spans so extensive a domain as this one. An example is colonial territory; once an important status attribute, it came to be a matter of little importance after the Second World War and at present may almost be considered as *detracting* from status. A second problem is that status attributes which *do* possess more universal applicability may be very difficult to operationalize. Here we may mention economic advantage; not only is such status a complex product of a wide variety of national attributes and environmental opportunities,[2] but its components vary markedly over time and space, rendering comparability difficult.

Fortunately, there is one status attribute which has been the subject of close and systematic scrutiny: the importance attributed to a nation by the other state members of the international system. Studies by Singer and Small (1966; 1970) have produced operational indicators of the reputational status enjoyed by all nation-members of the international system from 1817 to 1965. Of course, it may be argued that discrepancies involving reputational status will not be as important as those between capability and more concrete status benefits and rewards. But this is an empirical question; in the absence of hard evidence, there are two compelling arguments in favor of using attributed importance as a status dimension.

For one thing, it is clear that national decision-makers regard the recognition and reputational status granted them by the collective judgment of the system as an important reward in its own right. Most of the time, of course, they are not conscious of this recognition as a "reward" from other members of the international social system any more than most individuals would so regard their salary. That great powers should have a "place in the sun" in world estimation, and that smaller, weaker, and darker nations should be considered and treated as less important is so fundamental an assumption of the diplomatic culture that it needs no articulation; it is part of the way things "spozed to be." Its importance makes itself felt when a nation does not achieve a level of esteem and recognition consistent with its capabilities; if a great power is not invited to an important international conference, or a touring minister bypasses the local major power, or diplomatic recognition is systematically withheld from a large nation, a real sense of deprivation is felt immediately. If the source of this grievance is present for any extended period of time, it may make an important contribution to tension and hostility between nations, as the examples of interwar Germany and postrevolutionary China would seem to indicate.

But the importance of reputational status is not confined to mere diplomatic honor. There can be little question that there is a good deal of mutual interdependence between a nation's attributed status and its ability to obtain much more material rewards. Trade concessions, investment opportunities, military bases, colonies, alliance ties and other security arrangements, as well as many other concrete benefits accruing to a nation will in no small measure depend upon the importance attributed to that nation by the other members of the international system. At the same time reputational status itself will depend to some extent upon a nation's ability to obtain such material rewards; it is not only a status dimension in its own right, but also a reflection of a nation's position on other rankings. Attributed rank position is thus at once a product of previous social interaction which may in turn be an important factor in determining status on other dimensions in future interactions.

This is not to say, of course, that reputational status is necessarily a valid indicator of any other dimensions of national position, or even that discrepancies between capability and reputational status will necessarily prove to be the most important ones. The point being made is simply that the importance attributed to a nation by the other members of the system will have more than mere symbolic importance to the national actor concerned. If this is granted, it follows that inconsistencies between capability and attributed importance will produce even greater tensions than hitherto suggested. On the one hand, the nation whose reputational status is lower than its capability will perceive itself as suffering from material as well as symbolic deprivation, and, as suggested earlier, will be rather more likely to engage in hostile and aggressive behavior as a consequence. On the other hand, nations whose reputational status remains high while their capability declines may undertake quixotic actions rather than accept a loss status position and benefits. The behavior of the French in 1870, the Austrians in 1914, and the British in 1956 all seem to be examples of this "bellicose frivolity of senile empires" (Tuchman, 1962, p. 71).

The basic hypothesis of this study may thus be summed up as follows:

The greater the inconsistency between a nation's capabilities and the reputational status accorded it in the international system, the greater the likelihood that it will engage in conflict behavior.

Inconsistency and Conflict

Up until now we have focused on the similarities and differences between the international and domestic levels of analysis only as they apply to the selection of dimensions of status and forms of status inconsistency that are relevant to the international milieu. Left unexamined has been the process by which status rankings and inconsistencies affect a nation's conflict potential. In the case of the *individual*, we saw that discrepancies in his status set placed him under psychological stress, and that this stress might increase the probability of aggressive behavior. We have tacitly assumed that a similar tension-producing process takes place within *nations*. However, we must remember that nations are not individuals writ large, and that there is no a priori justification for assuming that a nation will perceive and act on status inconsistency in the same manner as an individual; the psychological and physiological processes associated with stress in the individual do not have plausible parallels at the national level. But not only must we steer clear of this implied anthropomorphism; we must also not assume that national decision-makers will experience frustration on behalf of their nation and so lead it in an aggressive direction. As many social scientists have pointed out, individual frustrations do not act directly on national behavior, but only on individual role performance (Singer and Ray, 1966; Rosenau, 1968; Kelman, 1965). To what extent this in turn affects policy outputs is a matter for empirical investigation. It behooves us, therefore, to examine in what ways status inconsistency may infringe upon national attitudes and behavior, and more generally, how it affects the probability of international conflict.

National Perception of Status Inconsistency

To begin with, the question may arise in what way nations "perceive" their status positions on different ranking dimensions. If we are speaking of the contemporary world, it is almost inconceivable that a nation's "attentive public," let alone its elite, should be in ignorance of its approximate place in the hierarchy. Even as early as the nineteenth century, it is unlikely that there was an actual dearth of information on these subjects amongst the policy elites of state members of the international system. We may more usefully direct our attention to the *salience* of this information to the elites. The assumption that elites, and the groups which support them, focus a good deal of attention on their nation's position on various status dimensions rests in turn on three further assumptions.

The first of these is that such "status strivings" are supported, or at least tolerated, by the rest of the society in normal periods. But, during times of civil disorder, crisis, or economic hardship, tolerance may be withdrawn from such elite activities. Moreover, in many smaller and poorer nations without extensive resources, or where techniques of mass mobilization are not available to elites, such tolerance and support may never have been generated in the first place. However, there is a good deal of evidence to suggest that under normal circumstances the attentive publics will give full support to their nation's status strivings in the international system either because they obtain vicarious gratification from doing so or because it is the social norm. Even during the twentieth century, withdrawal of public support for foreign policy has been regarded as an unusual event, and one which has implications for the security of tenure of the elite itself. If anything, the wider involvement of interest groups and mass publics may have *increased* the pressure on decision-makers to engage in such behavior; in the process of mobilizing support from these groups, political elites create a domestic payoff structure "full of rewards for continuing to feed the hostility and jingoism of the citizenry, and loaded with penalties if they fail to do so" (Singer and Ray, 1966, p. 306).

Second, we must assume that the nation in question interacts with its coevals to a degree sufficient for them to be perceived as "relevant others," and consequently to permit status comparisons with them as a referent system. Even in the nineteenth century, few nations were totally isolated from such inter-actions, and certainly the level of interaction within the core of the modern nation-state system has been very high for centuries. Nonetheless, even today status comparison may not involve the entire international system as a reference group (Russett, 1967; Galtung, 1966). Instead, most of the smaller nations, and indeed many of the larger ones, will tend to view their status in the context of a regional subsystem. The U.A.R. will probably make status comparisons with Israel or Iraq; it is very unlikely she will do so with Brazil or Norway, at least on the dimensions we employ in this study.

A final assumption is that the culture and political system of the nation are such as to produce psychic and political rewards for such a pursuit of status. At the present time, only the most peripheral nations—for example, Burma and Nepal—conduct their affairs with little regard for their global position, and the norm amongst the larger nations is one of extremely sensitive concern. However, it should not be forgotten that this was not always so, and that concern for status position has varied quite considerably amongst even major nations. The best example is the United States, which had little concern for its global position until the end of the nineteenth century.

The fact that the foregoing assumptions do not always hold should lead us to exercise considerable care in applying our hypothesis to the international system in an indiscriminate fashion. Status inconsistency will probably not be an important factor in contributing to conflict on the part of small, peripheral nations; it will be significant only when dealing with groups of nations engaged in fairly continual, intense status competition. In examining the hypothesis, it is therefore very important to select a test population made up of such "high interaction" nations.

The Effects of Inconsistency

Having examined the ways in which nations may or may not *perceive* status discrepancies, we turn now to the question of how they are likely to *react* to them. One possibility is that they will react in a fashion analogous to status inconsistent individuals, resorting either to withdrawal or to aggressive behavior if the inconsistent position is salient and continues for any length of time. The historical examples of status inconsistent nations cited previously point to this possibility. Yet (assuming for the moment that an association between status inconsistency and conflict has been demonstrated), there is no reason to suppose that discrepancies will lead to violence by stimulating aggression directly in this way. Such an assumption once again presumes too much on the analogy between the individual and the nation state. To the extent that decision-makers consider it a major priority to reduce or eliminate such discrepancies, frustration and hostility might indeed develop if the status inconsistent situation is prolonged. Nonetheless, this remains an empirical question, and in fact other "causal paths" at least as plausible will be discussed at length in the concluding chapters. For example, it is quite likely that the status inconsistent nation has greater difficulty in correctly assessing its own position in the hierarchy, and as Gulick (1956) points out in his study of the classical balance of power system, incorrect assessments of national rank-position may lead to a dangerous sense of false security or an optimistic forecast of success in aggressive designs. In either case ill-conceived policies threatening the peace will result. It is also plausible that the predominant reaction to status inconsistency will not be frustration and anger but insecurity and fear, emotions which are also likely to lead to conflict if a competitive quest for security develops within the system. A third alternative is that status inconsistency may lead to the realignment of nations in alliances and security agreements, which may in turn result in more war-prone configurations.

Of course there is little purpose to be served in examining these and other possibilities in detail prior to establishing that there *is* a relationship between status inconsistency and conflict. The point is that the discovery of a bivariate relationship between status inconsistency and war does not commit one to a simplistic "frustration-aggression" hypothesis or indeed to any particular config-uration of intervening variables. Exactly what these variables may prove to be must remain a matter to be determined by this and other studies.

Status Inconsistency and Status Rankings:
The Problem of Spuriousness

If the question of intervening variables can await an interpretation of the results, the possibility that any observed relationship may be spurious cannot be ignored. It may be that some third variable, closely associated with status inconsistency, is the actual cause of conflict, and that any observed correlation between status inconsistency and conflict is only an artifact of this association. This possibility is very important in the present case, since theoretical considerations allow us to identify several variables which might play such a role. Status inconsistency is defined in terms of two or more hierarchies in the international system, and so presumably will be closely associated statistically with other variables defined with reference to hierarchy. It could therefore be argued quite plausibly that they, and not status inconsistency, are causally related to war. A list of the possibilities would include such "theory-rich" variables as the rates of upward and downward mobility in military capability, level of economic development, prestige status, and the size of gaps or differentials between nations on these basic status indicators. It would therefore be foolhardy to rule out a priori the possibility of spuriousness. Of course, since the many possible relationships between international hierarchy and national behavior have only begun to be explored, it is hardly feasible to examine *all* such variables. But there are two which are of particular importance to the present effort: status position and status mobility.

Status Position and the Identification Problem

We have hypothesized that status inconsistency will be related to conflict behavior, but it is more than likely that status *position* by itself will also be so related. Even a quick glance at the data will show that the large and powerful nations are also the most war prone. Since status inconsistency is related to status position, there is a danger that any observed relationship may be spurious. We must therefore attempt to separate out the effects of the three variables from one another before we can arrive at any firm conclusions.

Following normal procedure in such cases, we might try to find the partial correlation between the independent variables and war—what effect has status inconsistency or mobility on conflict, holding constant for status position? Unfortunately, this procedure will not work. Blalock (1966, 1967a) has demonstrated that it is not possible to separate out the effects of these variables—in mathematical language, to identify the model—without making a priori assumptions about their direction and relative magnitude. In the case of status inconsistency, this may be readily demonstrated by writing the hypothesized relationships in regression form as follows: Let W be national war involvement, S_1 capability rank, S_2 attributed status rank, and S_3 the inconsistency between them. We may now write

$$W = a + b_1 S_1 + b_2 S_2 + b_3 S_3 + u \tag{2.1}$$

where a is the intercept, u the unexplained or "error term" variance and the b's are the regression slopes. Recall that status inconsistency was defined as a function of the difference between the two status positions. Thus,

$$S_3 = S_1 - S_2 \qquad\qquad (2.2)$$

If 2.1 and 2.2 are true their sum must be true, so

$$W = a + (b_1 + 1)S_1 + (b_2 - 1)S_2 + (b_3 - 1)S_3 + u \qquad (2.3)$$

Comparing 2.1 and 2.3, we see them to be identical save for the regression coefficients. In other words, at least two different sets of regression coefficients are compatible with a single equation generated from only one set of data, and there is therefore no empirical way of deciding which values are most satisfactory without making further assumptions or adducing additional information. Moreover, we may multiply 2.2 by any value prior to adding it to 2.1, so that there are in fact an infinite number of values of b_1, b_2 and b_3 which will satisfy 2.1. In other words, there is no technique that allows us to separate out the effects of status inconsistency (b_3) from the effects of capability and attributed status (b_1 and b_2).

Since these deductions may seem rather paradoxical, it is worth formulating this point in nonmathematical language. If S_1 and S_2 are a nation's capability and attributed status positions expressed in standardized units, then a nation's status inconsistency score is ($S_1 - S_2$). Now to separate out the effects of simple status position, we wish to observe the variation in war produced by allowing $S_1 - S_2$ to vary while holding status position constant. This is equivalent to saying "allow ($S_1 - S_2$) to vary, while holding S_1 and S_2 constant." Clearly, we cannot do this; such an injunction makes no sense.

There appear to be two ways around this difficulty. The first is to place a priori restrictions on the coefficients. If, for example, b_1 or b_2 were assumed to be zero, the model would be identifiable. Unfortunately, we do not have any good theoretical basis for making assumptions as strong as this about our data, nor would it be easy to decide empirically *which* coefficient should be zero since the two status variables will almost certainly show a high degree of association over the population of nations as a whole. Blalock (1967b) has shown that it is sometimes possible to determine the existence of a status inconsistency effect by making assumptions only about the direction of the coefficients. However, as might be expected, these weak assumptions result in rather weak evidence; using Blalock's method one can determine only the *existence* of such an effect, not its magnitude or importance. This is only partially satisfactory, even for the purpose of testing bivariate relationships, and it renders impossible any multivariate analysis including status inconsistency.

Fortunately, there is another way around this dilemma; we may test the hypotheses at the level of the international system as a whole. Instead of measuring the degree of association between national status inconsistency and war involvement across a population of individual nations, we may determine the relationship between the amount of status inconsistency in the *entire system* and the amount of war experienced by all nations. To return to the notation used in the equations above, our hypothesized relationship is no longer between W and S_3, but between $\sum W$ and $\sum S_3$ summed over the system as a whole. In defining our variables this way, the identification problem is avoided. Assuming that S_1 and S_2 are rank-positions, $\sum S_1$ and $\sum S_2$ will be constants for any given system size while of course $\sum W$ and $\sum S_3$ can vary. This removes the confounding "main effects," as status inconsistency is no longer a linear combination of these variables.

This is not to say, of course, that status position and status inconsistency are no longer mathematically related. However, instead of being defined as the difference between status positions, status inconsistency can be envisaged at the system level as the inverse of the degree of association between the capability and reputational rankings. If only a few nations have inconsistent statuses, the two orderings will match closely and thus be highly correlated. Conversely, if many are inconsistent, the two rankings will diverge, being associated only weakly over the population of nations.

It is proposed, then, to reformulate our hypothesis as follows:

The greater the amount of status inconsistency in the international system as a whole, the greater the level of conflict that will be experienced within it.

The Level of Analysis: Some Further Considerations

Mathematical difficulties with the variables are not the only reasons for testing the hypotheses at the system level. While war and peace are matters of national policy, it does not follow that war involvement is best explained at the level of the nation-state. It is a truism that such involvement is often due to events beyond the control of national decision-makers, but the point may be made much more generally: the sequence of interactions and decisions which leads to war, even the very disposition to enter conflict, may be the product of forces outside the control of any single national participant. To the extent that this is so, there will be little observed association between national attributes and war involvement, but there *will* be a high level of association between the appropriately-defined system attributes and the level of international violence characterizing the system as a whole. In short, testing hypotheses about international conflict at the level of the system as a whole should not be considered an inherently less valuable activity than the testing of similar propositions at the national level.

Of course, it *is* only an assumption, and not an established fact, that a good proportion of the variation in the amount of international war can be explained in this fashion. And, just as a national level test does not always shed light on the situation at the level of the system as a whole, so no demonstration at the system level can be interpreted as evidence of the ability of an hypothesis to explain the differences in war involvement from state to state (Robinson, 1950). This is a threefold liability.

First, while our theoretical interest with regard to many violent conflicts—particularly the global ones—lies with the conditions in the international system which gave rise to them, we are also interested in the differing degrees of aggressiveness displayed by nation-states. For although the responsibility for many wars must be shared by a number of states, most of us would refuse to abandon the belief that some conflicts are due to the aggressive policies of individual nations. To test only at the system level therefore introduces a definite value bias; in assuming that most of the variance can be explained at the system level, it tends to downplay the responsibility of the nation-state. One may or may not object to this according to one's particular world-view, but the point is that this assumption cannot be tested unless *both* levels of analysis are examined.

Second, considering the hypotheses at the system level makes difficult the measuring and testing of models containing intervening variables. As was mentioned earlier, it is very unlikely that status inconsistency and mobility will issue immediately in conflict. The nations involved (whether these be the inconsistent and mobile nations themselves or those which interact with them) must first *perceive* the existence of a discrepancy. Given the well-documented reluctance of statesmen to part with conventional wisdom, this may involve a good deal of time and several interaction sequences, and the interval between the fact and perception of it may vary from nation to nation. Then presumably behaviors, interactions, and relationships are altered in some fashion to deal with this; alliances are made and broken, patterns of trade altered, military capacity acquired, and tension begins to wax high, resulting eventually in violent conflict. In other words, at some point (and perhaps at many points) in the causal sequence leading from status inconsistency or mobility to war, we will need to examine the *national responses* to the stimulus; in tracing out the intervening variables, the metaphors of the national level appear almost mandatory and measurement at the system level correspondingly awkward.

Finally, a test confining itself to the system level will inevitably be less useful in a practical policy sense. To identify a high level of status inconsistency or mobility in the system with interstate war is of little immediate utility, at least by comparison with findings identifying the conditions under which *nations* become more war-prone. It does not help a decision-maker to inform him that there is a high probability of war somewhere in the world in the next five years; in fact, he may be excused for replying that little information has been imparted! At the very least, policy recommendations based on system level findings will be at a very high level of generalization. This is a serious criticism, as the subject matter of this study is oriented by its very nature not merely to explanation and prediction but also to control.

Despite all, it seems worthwhile to proceed with the system level test for the

C. L. HARDY LIBRARY
ATLANTIC CHRISTIAN COLLEGE
WILSON, N. C. 27893

present, given the relatively unexplored character of the field as it now stands. As theory building in international relations proceeds, and as evidence connecting status and conflict accumulates, stronger assumptions of the type proposed by Blalock may become possible. Once these can be made, identifying the coefficients is a straightforward matter. But progress in this direction will not develop *sui generis*, nor as the result of the purely speculative reasoning often labelled "theory" in international relations, but rather by the cumulative development of a body of empirical generalizations about the international system. In this sense, the present effort may indeed prove fruitful to future examination of the inconsistency hypothesis at the national level. For example, if it should transpire that the amount of status inconsistency in the international system is closely associated with the amount of war, and that there is little association between war and mobility on at least one of the status hierarchies, it would not be unreasonable to estimate the parameters at the national level by assuming that the association between status inconsistency and war is positive and that one of the status hierarchies has no direct effect.

Status Mobility—An Additional Confounding Influence

If national status *position* is likely to be closely associated with status inconsistency, so too is status mobility. Galtung (1964) has pointed out that amongst the most likely sources of status inconsistency are differences in national *rates of growth* on the demographic, economic, and military dimensions of power potential. If a nation experiences relatively rapid growth on these dimensions and thereby requires a higher capability status, it is unlikely that a corresponding rise in reputational status will occur immediately, making a temporary discrepancy almost inevitable. Moreover, the more rapid the growth, the larger the gap is likely to become, and the more slowly it may close.

We would therefore expect such differences in rates of growth to be closely associated with status inconsistency and thus an indirect cause of conflict. But it is quite possible that differential changes in capability lead to conflict in quite different ways. For one thing, many theorists believe that widening capability gaps among nations play an important role in the generation of conflict either by threatening an existing distribution of power, (Morgenthau, 1967, p. 204) or by rendering defenseless those who are downwardly mobile (Lagos, 1963, Chapter 1). It has also been suggested that under some conditions different national rates of change on these dimensions lead to the narrowing of capability differentials amongst the larger powers, and that this results in challenges to the international status quo and increased conflict (Organski, 1968, Chapter 14). In these examples, it is differential changes in capability and not status inconsistency that were causally connected with war.

A similar line of reasoning may be offered with regard to rates of change on the reputational status dimension. Here, too, differential change is likely to be associated with status inconsistency—negatively insofar as this change occurs in response to change in capability, and positively if induced by exogenous factors. Once again, we may hypothesize a direct causal connection between such differential change and conflict without reference to status inconsistency. As with any constant-sum attribute, upward mobility for some implies downward mobility for others, and there is little evidence that most nations readily acquiesce in obtaining a declining share of recognition, prestige, or other benefits they have acquired as the result of their importance in the eyes of their national coevals.

Given these arguments, it would scarcely be legitimate to ignore the impact of status mobility or to dismiss it with mere speculative reasoning. Therefore, the role of differential status mobility between and among nations in the interstate system will be explored by testing an additional hypothesis:

The greater the differences among national rates of change on the capability and reputational status dimensions, the greater the probability of conflict in the system.

Having now set out the basic hypotheses of the book, the next task is to devise appropriate procedures to test them.

Notes

1. In many places throughout this book, it will be necessary for reasons of style or clarity to refer to nations in terms which are, strictly speaking, appropriate only to individuals, e.g., as behaving, experiencing, expecting, or believing. As will be made amply clear below, the reader should not infer that anthropomorphism is intended; in all cases where it is not made explicit by the context, "nation" should be read as synonymous with "national foreign policy decision-makers and their influential clientele and subelites."

2. Those often cited include access to raw materials, markets, cheap labor, and investment opportunities, as well as many different aspects of international structure. For a thorough discussion of the complexities involved, see Hirschman (1969).

3 The Variables

The Spatial–Temporal Domain

The time span chosen to test these two hypotheses comprises the period from 1825 to 1964. Although the raw data were available from 1820 on, the necessity of computing the time rate of change from the previous period means that the observations begin with 1825. Nor are the data quite continuous; the 1945-9 period was reluctantly omitted after it was found impossible to collect information on most nations immediately after World War II. Nevertheless, the time segment examined is sufficiently large to avoid the risk of producing results which reflect only the short-run idiosyncracies of a particular period.

After some hesitation, it was decided to collect data on each of the variables at intervals of five years. On the one hand, this decision to employ such widely-spaced observations did of course reduce the "effective N" (the number of sets of observations) of the study, weakening the inferences to be made from the data. Furthermore, to the extent that significant fluctuations in the data values occurred *within* a given five-year period, questions might be raised about the reliability of the results. On the other hand, such a procedure was necessary to render manageable the task of data collection. Not only is the sheer *volume* of information to be collected thereby reduced, but five-year collection intervals bring the information gathering effort into line with governmental practice; for most of the period under study, published national statistics are updated only at fairly infrequent intervals. Moreover, it is doubtful if much distortion was introduced by this decision, since the rate of change in most variables was so slow as to render superfluous more closely spaced measurement intervals.

This brings us to an important issue always raised by studies employing very large and heterogeneous empirical domains. To what degree will the results obtained by analyzing the body of data as a whole reflect the relationships within smaller temporal segments? It is surely unwise to assume that the relationship between mobility, inconsistency, and war has remained unchanged over the entire period under study. It is not at all implausible, for example, that status inconsistency is not as disturbing an influence on the contemporary international system as it was when the relationships between nations were more formalized and conceptions of honor and prestige played a greater role in world affairs. On the other hand, it would not be surprising if changes in military capacity had a more unsettling effect in the latter part of the 140 year period than earlier on, given the threat posed by the various new advances in military technology.

29

Because of the relatively small number of widely spaced observations, it is not possible to examine the relationships in very small subsets of the data if we wish to obtain results which inspire any degree of confidence. However, it *is* possible to select smaller temporal domains which represent the earlier and later parts of the period as a whole. Thus, in addition to the analysis run on the entire 140 years, the periods 1825-1919, 1825-1944, and 1850-1964 will be examined separately.

The process of selecting an appropriate test population of nations is still more complex. As was indicated in the previous chapter, status inconsistency cannot be expected to influence the behavior of nations which scarcely interact with each other. For this reason, a meaningful test of the hypothesis requires the selection of a system or subsystem of nations whose members engage in frequent and important political interaction.

Ideally this process of selection should be undertaken on the basis of actual readings of the level of interaction between and among the various nations of the international system, as measured by such indicators as trade, diplomatic exchanges, alliances, and organizational memberships. While such a task is worthy indeed of attention from international politics scholars, it clearly represents a major effort of data collection and analysis in its own right, and hence cannot be attempted here. The problem, then, is to find a less elaborate method of selecting a highly interacting subset of the international community of nations.

For the first century of the period under examination, such a selection has already been made. In their pioneering article identifying the fluctuating state population of the international system from 1815 to 1945, Singer and Small (1966, p. 241) also identified a subpopulation or "central system," comprising "the most active or influential nations" as determined by the consensus of historians. Upon examination, this "central system" appears to consist of precisely those nations engaged in continuous, salient political interaction with one another.

However, Singer and Small distinguish between "central" and "peripheral" systems only until 1920, which fact forces us to adopt some substitute method for selecting the test population in the eight five-year periods between 1920 and 1964. During this time span the test population will comprise those nations which received diplomatic representatives from at least thirty percent of the other nations in the system. Exceptions were made in those few cases where the application of this threshold would have resulted in the exclusion of an acknowledged major power; China and the Soviet Union have been the prime examples. In practice, the thirty percent rule excludes chiefly two groups of nations: isolates such as Nepal, Yemen, and Mongolia, and states whose foreign policy is under the de facto control of another power, such as the British Commonwealth in the 1920s.

The Dependent Variable: International War

The measures of international conflict employed here are indices of the severity and magnitude of international war. While war is not, of course, the only variety of interstate conflict, and while it is not likely to be an immediate result of fluctuations in broad-guage structural variables such as those examined here, it is one of the most important and, at the same time, most easily measured form of such conflict. Alternative measures of conflict, such as "threats" or "negative sanctions" suffer both from low reliability and unavailability of data for all but the most recent periods. The data on international war is that of Singer and Small (1972), and while the coding rules governing its collection are to be found in that volume, a summary is in order here.

To begin with, not all violent conflicts between states qualify as wars. For a conflict to be included, at least one participant must be a state member of the international system. This means that not only interstate wars, but also colonial or imperial conflicts where only one side is a recognized state are included. The inclusion of both "intrasystemic" and "extrasystemic" wars is designed to ensure that a nation's *entire* international war experience is measured. To exclude colonial and imperial conflicts would seriously distort the actual war experience record of such nations as Britain, which fought twelve colonial and imperial wars in this 140 years, and only seven against other state members of the system. One cannot argue that combat against Europeans constitutes war involvement whereas conflicts with other peoples do not.

On the other hand, civil conflicts of all descriptions are *excluded*, along with wars between and among entities which are not state-members of the system. Although other nations often become involved in civil wars directly or indirectly, and although some conflicts during this period between nonstate entities possess many of the characteristics of international war,[1] the purpose of the present exercise is to predict to violent conflict directly involving nation-states. This does not imply, of course, that the extension of our hypotheses to other units may not be valid; the rationale behind the restriction is simply the need to insure, for purposes of *this* test, that we are dealing with a more or less homogeneous group of actors and conflicts.

To be included as wars, violent conflicts had to meet an additional requirement in the form of a threshold of *severity*. Intrasystemic conflicts must have involved at least one thousand battle fatalities on both sides, excluding civilian deaths and those caused by disease and famine. In the case of extrasystemic violence, the *state-member* involved must suffer at least one thousand battle deaths. In other words, "wars" include only conflicts of some physical magnitude, and exclude skirmishes, border incidents, and the like. Such a threshold enhances both validity and reliability; it makes little sense to term very minor violent clashes "wars," and completing a list of all such skirmishes, to say nothing of obtaining accurate data on them, would prove an awesome task.

Applying these coding rules, Singer and Small find eighty-nine international wars between 1825 and 1964. Since mere frequency is hardly a sensitive indicator of either the *amount* or the *duration* of war occurring in the international system, two other indices constructed by these authors are used. One is an indicator of war *magnitude*, measured by the number of "nation-months" of war experienced. The second is an indicator of the severity of war, the number of battle fatalities as defined above. To render the data comparable to that collected on the other variables, each nation's war experience was aggregated by five-year periods so that the total number of nation-months and battle deaths arising from war involvement *begun* in each five-year period was included in the total for that period.

The Independent Variables (I):
Capability Status

Now that we have specified the empirical domain to be examined, and outlined the coding rules for the dependent variable, war, it remains to operationalize the independent variables—differences in national rates of status mobility, and status inconsistency. In Chapter 2 it was hypothesized that conflict would arise from inconsistency between, or rapid mobility on, two main rank dimensions: capability and reputational status. The problem, then, is how to produce operational indicators for these.

Possible indicators of capability are many and varied, and there is little compelling evidence which would lead us to choose any one simple indicator of capability. One solution to this difficulty has been the creation of a *combined* index of national capability. Rather than choosing an index representing only one of the contributing factors, adherents of this approach have attempted by a variety of techniques to produce a single index of capability combining all relevant factors. Examples of such attempts are to be found in articles by German (1960) and Fucks (1965). The former produced an index combining twenty-five separate measures of demographic, economic, and military potential; the latter produced an index based essentially on population and steel production. Both of these approaches suffer from important disadvantages. The German method ensures the inclusion of all relevant factors, but at the expense of discrimination; the thorny problem of assigning weights to the various contributing elements is settled in a totally arbitrary fashion. Moreover, his computations depend on the availability of data on a number of very sophisticated indicators, and this rules out their application to much of the empirical domain under consideration here. By contrast, Fucks' index requires data on only two variables, population and steel production, and these are relatively easy to come by. Moreover, Fucks evinces far more concern with the relationship between the components of his index and their changes over time, a critical concern in a study spanning 140 years. Nonetheless, his index has serious validity problems; most notably, it omits all reference to military capability, and in so doing becomes largely a measure of economic capability weighted by sheer population size.

Surveying these and other experiences with the construction of a composite index, it is not difficult to come to the conclusion that the generation of a satisfactory combined index of capability will require a great deal of further empirical research on the relationships among the various constituent indicators—such as that begun by Shinn (1969)—as well as an examination of the relationships between these indices and the outcomes of influence attempts in the international system. Since this task is well beyond the scope of the present effort, an alternative approach is used here. It was decided to employ a number of very simple indices, each representing an important component or facet of demographic, industrial, or military capability. Throughout the ensuing calculations, these indices will be considered as *alternative* measures of power capability and utilized separately. Only after the bivariate relationships between status mobility, status inconsistency, and war have been determined will the indices be "combined" by means of multivariate statistical techniques.

To decide to use multiple indicators is easier than to develop a set of measures which adequately cover the broad spectrum encompassed by power capability. In every case, it was necessary to balance two competing requirements: to maximize the indices' proximity to the concepts they purport to measure, and to use measures for which adequate data can be obtained. After due consideration, it was decided to employ five indices of demographic, industrial, and military capability.

The first index used is *total population*. While gross population is no longer—if indeed it ever was—the most important factor in national capability, it still remains central to a nation's position in the hierarchy. As Organski (1968, p. 144) points out, all of the world's major powers have more than 50 million people, and the superpowers both exceed 200 million. Moreover, it is probably the indicator with the best overall reliability; whatever statistics governments keep, they usually begin with a census.

The population data presented here are obtained from two main sources. After the second World War, figures from the U.N. DEMOGRAPHIC YEARBOOK (1947-1967) are used exclusively. Prior to the war, data were obtained from the ALMANACH DE GOTHA, (1815-1942) occasionally supplemented by the STATESMAN'S YEARBOOK (1864-1964) and various monographic sources.[2] There are, of course, reasons to be skeptical of many figures reported by these sources. There is a noticeable tendency to rely heavily on official information; not only are many national census figures obtained by unreliable methods, but systematic bias cannot always be ruled out since, for electoral and other reasons, census results often have political meaning. Wherever possible, alternative sources and estimates were used to check doubtful or seemingly inconsistent figures, but it should be noted that genuinely independent verification was not possible except in a tiny minority of cases.

The second index is also demographic: *urban population.* For present purposes, "urban" is defined as any city with over twenty thousand people; this is designed to exclude towns which are essentially suburbs or market centers for rural areas, and to include only populations engaged in activities and possessed of a life-style that is nonagricultural. The cut-off figure is, of course, a compromise; authorities do not agree on where the line should be drawn. The U.N. uses one-hundred thousand as a threshold, but this is far too high for the nineteenth century since it excludes even major centers such as Toronto before 1880. On the other hand, it may be that twenty thousand is far too low for the present day; in the age of the automobile, a town this size is not usually considered "urban." Ideally, a variable threshold would seem called for, but once again the construction of such an index would be a major project of itself. Thus, the twenty thousand figure used by ALMANACH DE GOTHA was employed throughout the period under study. While this is somewhat arbitrary, the purpose of such an index is not to achieve demographic precision but to provide a more sensitive indicator of mobilizable population resources than gross population. Urban population figures, even when constructed this crudely, tend to separate out that portion of a nation's population which possesses the melange of technical and organizational skills we refer to as "modern," and as such should provide a better reflection of a nation's power capability. As with the total population index, the chief data sources were ALMANACH DE GOTHA and the U.N. DEMOGRAPHIC YEARBOOKS.

It would be quite easy to conceive of additional, more refined demographic indicators. For example, a more valid measure of the gross demographic resources available to a regime might be the proportion of men in the productive (and military) age bracket, usually measured as the number between eighteen and fifty years of age. The level of skills in the population might better be indicated by that proportion of the population engaged in "modern" occupations. Unfortunately, data for these variables, while readily available from U.N. sources for the post-World War II period, are unobtainable for all but a handful of nations prior to 1945. Moreover, even were they available, the difficulties in constructing indices comparable over time would preclude their use, given our present state of knowledge; the mix of skills comprising mobilizable population resources has varied markedly over time (Kuznets, 1965, p. 106-7). With widely varying and rapidly changing rates of mortality and morbidity, it would even be difficult to set age limits for the "active" population; in societies with advanced medical care, fifty is far too low, but it is probably too high for many less developed nations.

If refined indices raise difficulties in the area of demographic capability, it is in the field of economic capacity that the task of constructing valid indices seems to be the most complex. Combined measures of economic capacity such as gross national product are of course ruled out for reasons of data availability, but difficulties extend to far simpler indicators. For example, gross industrial energy consumption is an excellent measure of modern industrial production, but it clearly tells us little about the capability of preindustrial economies. Another possible index is food production, a crucial material resource and particularly important in time of war. However, even quite early in the nineteenth century, food production in many countries depended as much on the demands of trade as on domestic needs, and, conversely, many of the most prosperous nations (such as Britain) imported much of their food.

It was finally decided to measure economic capability by iron and steel production. Although the growth of some industry can and has proceeded independently of the growth of steel production, and while historically the process of industrialization has seldom *begun* with the acquisition of such a capacity, the two have virtually everywhere been closely associated in the process of economic development (Fucks, 1965). Moreover, iron and steel production (albeit of a cruder type) is in many ways central to the technology of even a preindustrial economy. Not only are iron and steel consumed in the domestic economy, but they are obviously crucial to weapons manufacture.

Our measure, then, is production measured in metric tons. To compensate for changing technology, crude (pig) iron production is used from 1825 to 1895, and crude steel production thereafter. Data are readily available from DE GOTHA for nineteenth century iron production, and the United Nations has relatively complete statistics on twentieth century steel production. Not all nations in the test population are mentioned in these sources, but in all cases checks confirmed that their absence was due to the fact that they produced little or no iron or steel.

However, these omissions could, under some circumstances, constitute a major disadvantage for the index, rendering it relatively insensitive at the lower end of the scale; while it discriminates well amongst the major powers, it cannot distinguish amongst the many nonproducing nations. In the present study this difficulty is somewhat attenuated by the above-noted omission of many smaller nations, and hence iron and steel production was deemed a satisfactory measure of economic capability for present purposes.

The third major component of national capability to be included is national military capacity. While it may be argued that, in the last analysis, military capability is a direct function of a nation's demographic and economic resource base, (Organski, 1968, pp. 112-3) this would seem to be true only during all-out war, when a substantial fraction of a nation's resources is committed to the military sector. Under other circumstances, military capability will vary independently of the national resource base, with some nations (such as Germany and France before WWI) possessing large standing armed forces while others (such as the U.S. prior to World War II) rest content with force levels very low in relation to their demographic and industrial resources.

Once again, the need for reliable data comparable over a long period of time dictated the choice of a relatively simple index: the number of effectives possessed by each nation. For present purposes these are defined as regular or standing army, navy, air, and colonial forces. The index includes only the number of military personnel actually in uniform at any one time; specifically excluded are reserve or militia forces, despite the fact that for many nations these comprise a major portion of total armed strength.

The rationale behind this exclusion is the enhancement of comparability and reliability. The standard of training and armament in the reserves varies enormously from nation to nation. During the nineteenth century, the reserves of the continental powers were vastly superior in these respects not only to the smaller and non-European nations, but also to nations such as Britain which relied on regular forces and whose reserves were scarcely trained at all. A further complication is the fact that most major nations have various "grades" of reserves, distinguished either by the amount of training in the British and American fashion, or by age as in Europe. While no solution to these difficulties of comparison is ideal, it was felt that the best compromise was to include only regular forces, where fewer ambiguities exist (Cassell, 1966, p. 12).

This is not to say that there are *no* ambiguous cases. One type of difficulty is caused by paramilitary police forces. Since this index was to include *all* regular troops who would actually be engaged in combat with other nations, these forces are included if they exist *in place* of an army as in Panama or Costa Rica, and excluded otherwise. By an extension of this principle, militia forces *are* included when they exist in lieu of a standing army as in Switzerland.

One final problem with this index occurs when the data collection date coincides with a war. Not only are wartime military figures often impossible to obtain, but they fluctuate enormously over very short periods of time. Moreover, if (as in 1870) only a few nations were at war, military force levels might not reflect the overall military balance. It was decided that, in all such cases, the data would be collected for the year immediately preceding the onset of war.

Despite difficulties with data availability, it was felt that the importance of the military dimension of capability warranted the construction of an alternative index. The number of military personnel is not necessarily related to military prowess, as it does not take into account such factors as weapons, material, and training. It thus tends to inflate the military strength of large, poor nations with sizeable but ineffective armies. To compensate for this it was decided to include data on armed forces expenditures on the assumption that the amount of money spent will partially reflect differences in per man effectiveness.

Data for this index consists of annual military expenditure figures as indicated in published military budgets, converted for comparability to sterling before 1920 and to dollars after that date, according to official exchange rates. Obviously, this way of proceeding could produce inaccuracies. First, no attempt was made to allow for defense costs hidden under other budget categories. Second, official exchange rates were used throughout, despite the fact that these often do not reflect a currency's real purchasing power. Moreover, even if the exchange rates are accurate in terms of *international* purchasing power, they do not reflect differing cost levels and pay scales from country to country; with the same number of U.S. dollars, Turkey can buy "more army" than the U.S. (Cassell, 1966, pp. 13-14). Nevertheless, it was felt that for an initial test this index was adequate, particularly as it is designed chiefly as a check on the military personnel indicator. Unfortunately, reliable military expenditure data are available only from 1850 onwards; thus, all calculations employing this index refer to a correspondingly truncated temporal domain.

Having thus developed five indices of capability status, let us now turn to the other major rank-dimension to be examined, attributed status.

The Independent Variables (II): Attributed Status

A nation has reputational status attributed to it by many groups and organizations both inside and outside its national borders. Under some circumstances these private evaluations of national importance may be of great salience to a nation, as for example when it wishes to float a bond issue or promote tourism or investment. But the evaluations of national importance normally of the greatest salience to any group of national decision makers will be those made by their counterparts in other nations. To produce an index of attributed national importance thus requires reconstructing these mutual evaluations over the 140 years under study from the traces available to us, and finding some means of combining the evaluations of many state actors in the system into a single index score for each nation.

No doubt there are as many different ways of doing this as there are traces of such evaluations. One possible approach might be an analysis of diplomatic documents and published statements in search of actual statements making such status comparisons. The original design of this research anticipated the construction of such an index from documents and newspapers of record. It was quickly determined, however, that neither statesmen nor journalists articulate their status evaluations unless the nation concerned is, for some reason, the focus of their attention, as for example in time of war or revolution. Given the enormous amount of time and effort that would have to be invested to collect and analyze these statements, and the unreliable nature of the scale which would result, it was decided not to proceed in this way.

A more promising avenue is to infer status attributions from the behavior of nations. While statesmen for many reasons do not make explicit their judgments of national importance, their actions towards other nations in the course of day-to-day diplomatic relations will reflect these judgments. For example, when international conferences are held to discuss matters of common concern to many members of the system, the nations which enjoy a relatively higher reputational status will stand a higher probability of being invited. One might also expect that such nations have a greater probability of being members of alliances and international organizations, since their membership in such groupings will be sought after by other members of the system. Thus, a number of indicators are possible based on various facets of international diplomatic interaction.

Following Singer and Small (1966), the index of attributed status used here is based on the number of diplomatic missions accredited to a nation's capital by the other state members of the international system. It was reasoned that, of the many national decisions which would be influenced by attributed importance, the most sensitive, comparable, and measurable would be decisions to send or not to send diplomatic representatives to the various national capitals. The use of a solitary index here is justified by the fact that there are fewer questions of index validity than in the case of the individual indices of power capability. As these authors note, an index based on the assignment of diplomatic representatives is in fact a combined one, since these decisions are "a reflection of a wide range of internal and external considerations affecting those responsible for deciding upon each such assignment" (1966, p. 240).

This is not to say that this index is free from possible sources of distortion. As only one possible example, different "diplomatic cultures" might produce misleading values. Latin American nations are alleged to place a great deal of emphasis on formal diplomacy, and thus may be prone to send—and receive—rather more missions that one would normally expect for nations of their size and influence. But for the present purpose this index seems especially suitable; as some of the above-mentioned examples of international status inconsistency seem to show (China being chief amongst them), diplomatic recognition appears often to be not merely an indicator of attributed status, but its very substance.

The basic Singer-Small data are used; this consists of information on the number and identity of all diplomatic missions at the ambassadorial, ministerial, and charge d'affaires levels present in each capital. Although there are slight unavoidable irregularities in the collection dates, in all cases the information was comparable with the rest of the data. However, the index is constructed in a slightly different fashion from the method originally employed by Singer and Small. Instead of using a complex procedure to weight the ranks of the missions received, it was decided to base each nation's importance score on only the *number* of missions. To control for the fact that the maximum number of missions that could be received varies with the population of the system, the raw score is normalized by the total *possible* number of missions, one less than the number of nations in the system. For selected test years, this much simplified index gave rank-order correlations of better than .95 with the original weighted status index (Singer and Small, 1970a).

Now that the operational procedures governing the collection of the raw data have been spelled out, we may turn to the methods used to transform and aggregate them into indices of status inconsistency and status mobility.

The Measurement of National Status Inconsistency

Up to this point, the concept of "inconsistency" or "discrepancy" has been left rather vague, and there are in fact several intuitively plausible ways of operationalizing it. Since the measurement procedures employed at this final stage of data generation will exert considerable influence on the results, it is necessary to explore the theoretical and practical advantages of the alternative procedures prior to making a choice among them.

According to one interpretation, status inconsistency may be said to exist when a nation's position on one status continuum is "high" while on another it is "low." This definition is favored by the sociologists in their studies of inconsistency in domestic society (Jackson, 1962; Lenski, 1954). Status position is divided into "high" and "low" (or, sometimes, high-medium-low), inconsistent individuals being those who have one status position below the line and one above. This procedure has several important disadvantages. First, it is not always clear exactly where to draw the line between high and low status. In some cases, a dichotomous categorization makes a good deal of sense (for example, white versus nonwhite), but when status is measured by means of a continuous variable, as is the case with the indicators of national status developed here, it may be quite difficult to find a natural "cutting point." Moreover, there is evidence to indicate that manipulation of the cutting point has altered the results of some studies (Kenkel, 1956).

Second, the use of dichotomous categorization severely limits the techniques of analysis which can be applied to the data. There are, of course, methods of determining the degree of association between pairs of dichotomous variables, but such powerful multivariate methods as causal analysis and path analysis cannot be used.

Finally, and most important, to force continuous variables into dichotomies is to throw away an enormous amount of information. If a social system had two status continua with as few as 12 different positions on them, there would be 132 possible status combinations which would be inconsistent. However, if the continua were dichotomized, only 60 of these would be scored as inconsistent. In general, the dichotomous method is sensitive only to gross discrepancies, and of course it does not distinguish between *degrees* of discrepancy. It may turn out upon investigation that such simplifications are justified, but this is an empirical question which cannot be answered prior to conducting the investigation itself. In short, this method does not appear to answer the needs of the present inquiry.

A second method would go to the opposite extreme and measure status inconsistency as a continuous variable (Midlarsky, 1969). Here the procedure would be to put national scores on the several dimensions in standard score form, then to measure status inconsistency as the difference of the two standard scores. This procedure has the advantage of making maximum use of the information available, and producing an interval level measure of status inconsistency. However, there are two concomitant disadvantages.

First, this procedure is sensitive to, and subject to distortion by, the *distribution* of national status positions on the dimensions in question. Putting the status positions in standard score form (thus ensuring that the distributions have the same mean and standard deviation) does not prevent distributions from having different *shapes*, and these can affect the status inconsistency scores. If the distribution on one dimension was negatively skewed while the other was positively skewed, the mean status inconsistency score will be somewhat larger than would have been the case had both distributions exhibited the same shape. This distortion is analogous to that which occurs in the computation of the product-moment correlation coefficient when the variables are not normally distributed (Johnston, 1963, pp. 207-11). As with the product-moment correlation, this sensitivity to distortion implies that only those variables whose distributions approximate normality should be used for computations of this type. Unfortunately, even a cursory glance at the data is enough to indicate that this condition is far from being met. Not only is there a good deal of skew, but its magnitude and direction change from variable to variable. It would appear, then, that this method is ruled out as well.

However, this is not necessarily a severe handicap. While national decision makers no doubt perceive intervals on most status scales (the prime example being military capability), they will likely be a good deal more attentive to rank position; indeed, status inconsistency is often referred to as "rank disequilibrium" (Galtung, 1964). This leads naturally to a third possible procedure for the measurement of status inconsistency, the one that will be adopted here. Instead of measuring it as the difference between a nation's standardized scores on two attributes, this procedure defines it as the difference between two *rank positions*. That is, if in comparison to the rest of the test population a nation ranks eighth in military personnel, but only twelfth on diplomatic importance, its status inconsistency score for that pair of dimensions is four.

This operational procedure is placed midway between the two outlined above, and appears to avoid the major difficulties of both. Unlike the dichotomous method, it is sensitive to relatively small discrepancies between status dimensions. On the other hand, since it does not depend upon the distribution of values on the status attributes, no distortion is introduced by extreme data values. Nor does it assume national sensitivity to extremely fine gradations on these attributes, but only an awareness on the part of national decision-makers as to which nations stand below them, and which are positioned above them, on the relevant dimensions of status.

Using this procedure, the inconsistency between each nation's *attributed* status and each of its five *capability* status scores is computed, producing five separate indices of status inconsistency.

The Measure of National Status Mobility

It would be possible to employ a similar rank-order procedure to compute the mobility of nations on the several status continua. That is, national mobility on a given dimension could be defined as the change in its rank-position over the five year interval between measurements. However, there is an important reason why this procedure is not the most appropriate one; it will not produce meaningful results when the size of the system changes between two observations. Changes in national rank-position can occur merely because other nations enter or leave the system. If, for example, additional nations near the middle of the hierarchy entered into the test population, those nations in the bottom quartile would experience "downward mobility" as measured by their rank on the status continuum. Obviously, this sort of rank-movement does not have the same theoretical purport as changes in rank-position within a numerically fixed system.

In this case, a more satisfactory index may be constructed using the raw status indicators rather than the rank-orderings. Unlike the case of status inconsistency, this does not involve comparing national positions on two differently distributed variables; here we are interested in rates of change in position on a single variable, and the shapes of the distributions of the indices change little over a five-year period. This permits us to use the raw data in interval level form without courting the danger that the resulting scores will be mere artifacts.

Specifically, the first step in constructing indices of national mobility is to compute the time rates of change on each variable for each nation. The most common procedure for doing this—taking the *percentage* rate of change from time t to time $t + 5$—was *not* employed, since in percentage change calculations the denominator of the calculation reflects only the *first* of the two raw data values, and has no maximum upper value. If, however, the absolute change is normalized by the *sum* of the two data values, not only are the values of both observations taken into account in the normalization process, but the resulting index now varies between zero and one. The second step is to standardize the indices; we are not interested in each nation's time rate of change by itself, but only in how the different national scores vary relative to one another. To obtain such a measure of *relative* change, we take the difference between the raw rate for each nation and the mean rate of change for the entire population of nations.

Transforming the Variables

The decision to test the hypothesis at the level of the system as a whole requires the specification of one final set of procedures; those whereby the variables are aggregated. In the case of international war, this presents no difficulty. The amount of war begun in the system as a whole at any given time is simply the sum of the amounts entered into by all the nations of the test population; the values for each five year period since 1825 are given in Table 3-1.

Status inconsistency can also be measured in this way, but here it is necessary

Table 3-1
Magnitude and Severity of National War Involvement Begun, 1825-1964

Period Beginning	Nation-Months of Involvement Begun	Battle Deaths from Involvement Begun (1000s)
1825	108.0	153.2
30	0.0	0.0
35	58.5	31.0
40	3.5	1.0
45	96.0	96.7
50	118.5	268.3
55	75.5	43.2
60	213.5	132.5
65	203.5	147.1
70	93.5	193.5
75	236.5	320.0
80	89.0	36.6
85	2.0	3.0
90	25.5	21.0
95	157.5	99.5
1900	39.0	130.0
05	30.0	12.0
10	496.5	7581.3
15	292.5	1248.0
20	58.5	25.0
25	36.5	8.0
30	105.0	190.0
35	584.5	5506.3
40	432.0	1064.7
50	605.0	1907.1
55	41.0	75.2
60	2.0	10.0

to normalize the resulting index, since the amount of status inconsistency that can occur in the international system is a nonlinear function of system size, specifically, a function of the sum of the integers from *1* to *n* where *n* is the number of states in the system (Galtung, 1966, pp. 181-7). Thus, the system-wide sum of status inconsistency was divided by $n^2 + n$, which is the sum of these integers multiplied by *2* to remove the constant term (Siegal, p. 203). The results are displayed in Table 3-2.

Table 3-2

Status Inconsistency in the International System, 1825-1964, Computed Between Attributed Diplomatic Importance and Five Indices of National Capability

Period Beginning	Total Population	Urban Population	Military Personnel	Military Expenditures	Iron/Steel Production
1825	.142	.195	.095		.166
1830	.022	.067	.084		.274
1835	.164	.155	.151		.173
1840	.169	.204	.213		.196
1845	.217	.213	.249		.236
1850	.182	.169	.196	.173	.209
1855	.164	.129	.182	.124	.164
1860	.187	.129	.173	.107	.169
1865	.129	.080	.155	.093	.164
1870	.124	.058	.111	.071	.200
1875	.071	.044	.102	.049	.133
1880	.097	.062	.145	.062	.138
1885	.114	.076	.121	.076	.128
1890	.142	.097	.138	.087	.111
1895	.205	.152	.177	.108	.172
1900	.220	.158	.175	.138	.128
1905	.197	.161	.172	.150	.134
1910	.213	.145	.227	.165	.124
1913	.221	.134	.244	.176	.122
1920	.269	.193	.250	.193	.266
1925	.261	.200	.242	.243	.245
1930	.223	.191	.240	.255	.210
1935	.243	.194	.216	.226	.226
1938	.308	.256	.308	.245	.215
1950	.241	.234	.283	.224	.198
1955	.237	.210	.290	.251	.243
1960	.226	.192	.222	.208	.177

Table 3-3

Differential Rates of Change on Six Status Attributes in the International System, 1825-1964

Period From-To	Total Population	Urban Population	Military Personnel	Military Expenditures	Iron/Steel Production	Diplomatic Importance
1820-25	.209	.151	.169		.231	1.908
1825-30	.014	.058	.018		.057	.296
1830-35	.216	.084	.156		.069	.396
1835-40	.017	.025	.291		.065	.079
1840-45	.015	.091	.105		.083	.096
1845-50	.011	.214	.139	.009	.339	.066
1850-55	.015	.047	.095	.143	.113	.098
1855-60	.011	.094	.143	.191	.122	.056
1860-65	.021	.053	.184	.244	.079	.057
1865-70	.013	.064	.123	.235	.086	.046
1870-75	.012	.036	.154	.198	.111	.052
1875-80	.024	.035	.047	.045	.072	.056
1880-85	.017	.004	.023	.009	.027	.017
1885-90	.028	.077	.149	.100	.088	.053
1890-95	.009	.048	.131	.103	.331	.050
1895-1900	.021	.051	.136	.101	.378	.066
1900-05	.045	.083	.211	.068	.234	.068
1905-10	.012	.057	.198	.111	.108	.217
1910-13	.051	.026	.209	.266	.145	.068
1913-20	.157	.196	.304	.432	.461	.190
1920-25	.003	.008	.021	.031	.029	.016
1925-30	.022	.068	.153	.219	.253	.077
1930-35	.036	.116	.181	.250	.347	.062
1935-38	.116	.080	.204	.259	.322	.114
1938-50	.057	.153	.334	.370	.286	.201
1950-55	.032	.048	.224	.376	.238	.155
1955-60	.026	.165	.193	.320	.353	.130

To aggregate the amount of status mobility in the system, a rather different procedure must be employed. Obviously, it is not possible to sum the national scores as derived above; since they are calculated as the difference between the national rates of change and the mean rate for the system as a whole, they will always sum to zero. But because the theoretical basis for including an index of mobility at the national level was to measure *differential* changes in capability and prestige, the appropriate index at the system level is one which measures not the total or the average system-wide increase, but rather the *variation* in the national changes throughout the system. This is done by taking the standard deviation of the national rates of change on the six basic status indicators for the test population. These values are to be found in Table 3-3.

This completes the operational definition of the variables to be used in the study. The way is now prepared for a consideration of the analytical techniques to be used in investigating the relationships between status mobility, status inconsistency, and international war.

Notes

1. Notable examples are the Baganda wars of expansion in early nineteenth century East Africa. See Ingman (1957, pp. 18-9).

2. A full list of data sources for all indices of the independent variable is to be found in the Appendix.

4 Data Analyses and Results

Introduction

Having generated data on both the dependent and independent variables, we may now turn to an examination of the statistical relationships among status mobility, status inconsistency, and war in the post-Napoleonic international system. This examination will involve three analytic techniques: simple bivariate correlation, stepwise multiple regression, and dependence analysis. These are treated *ad seriatim* in the three sections of this chapter immediately following; in each case, the analytic procedures and their rationale are spelled out, followed by description of the results obtained. Then, in a fourth and final section, the main findings are summarized; here the evidence both for and against the two central hypotheses of this study is set forth, along with their more crucial limiting conditions.

Bivariate Association

Product-Moment versus Rank-Order Statistics

The first and most basic decision to be made concerning data analysis is, which of the many techniques of bivariate association is most appropriate to the present study? Since the data are in the form of interval measurement scales, we might normally expect to use the product-moment measure of association, the Pearson *r*. However, as can be readily seen from Tables 3-1, 3-2, and 3-3, these data do not fulfill a crucial assumption of this statistic: that of normally distributed values. The correct method of measuring association between interval scales when this condition is not met continues to be the subject of considerable disagreement amongst data analysts.

Some contend that data sets which do not satisfy the assumption of normal distribution or which are subject to a good deal of measurement error can produce seriously biased correlation coefficients (Siegel, 1956). It is better, therefore, to use techniques which do not make such assumptions and which are relatively insensitive to measurement error; rank-order correlations are the conventional solution. Others argue that the sensitivity of product-moment coefficients is more than compensated for by the greater flexibility and ease of interpretation which they possess (Tufte, 1969). For one thing, they have an unambiguous theoretical interpretation; squaring the correlation coefficient gives us the amount of variance "explained," or accounted for, by the dependent variable.[1] In addition, the regression coefficients tell us the magnitude of the change in one variable produced by a given change in the other; in Blalock's words (1962, p. 51), they give us "the laws of science." This kind of interpretation cannot easily be applied to rank-order coefficients. Moreover, the latter cannot be readily used for purposes of multivariate analysis. One may obtain partial rank-order correlations, but such powerful techniques as multiple regression and path analysis require more stringent assumptions. In short, the amount of information which we can extract from the data is, as usual, directly proportional to the strength of the assumptions we are willing to make about it. As Coombs puts it: (1964, p. 5), "We buy information with assumptions—'facts' are inferences, and so also are data and measurement scales."

While the exploratory nature of this analysis precludes making many strong assumptions, the need for using multivariate techniques is obvious. Hence it was decided to compute both product-moment and rank-order descriptive statistics for purposes of comparison. When this was done, it became clear that most of our intuitive fears were ill-founded. The two types of statistical test yielded values of roughly the same magnitude, although, as might be expected, the rank-order coefficients were generally somewhat lower. Once it became reasonably clear that the choice of coefficient did not exert any important influence on the pattern of results, it was decided to avoid redundancy and report only the product-moment values.

Reported as well will be the statistical significance of the results. While of course the present data represent not a sample but a closed population, there are four reasons why it was felt useful to include them in the study. First, even in a closed population one may speak of the probability of a given correlation resulting from mere random fluctuation; the "level" of significance may be interpreted as that probability. Second, these values represent convenient *N-dependent* thresholds which allow us to decide whether the values obtained— taking into account both the magnitude of the coefficient and the size of the data base—are sufficiently large to allow reliable inferences to be made. Third, in a sense we *are* working with a sample; we are examining only a few of the possible indicators of war, status inconsistency, and status mobility, and use only several of many possible observation intervals, lags, and time-spans. More important, one hopes that these findings may be generalized to the even broader span of time both before and after the 140 years presently under study. Finally, whatever function these significance levels serve in the *bivariate* context, they play a crucial role in the multivariate analysis, as will be discussed in a later section.

The Results: Status Inconsistency

Turning first to the simple product-moment correlations between status incon- sistency and the amount of national war involvement, we find that when the various indices of the independent variable are used to predict to the number of nation-months and battle-deaths of war begun in the five-year period immediately following—that is to say, no time lag is employed—there seems to be definite evidence of a statistical association. As we see from Table 4-1, if we take the 140 year period as a whole, a moderate degree of association appears; 4 of the 8 correlations are significant at the .05 level, and 2 at the .01 level.

Table 4-1
Correlations Between Status Inconsistency and National War Involvement Begun

Period Lag		No Lag			5 Years			10 Years			15 Years	
		NM	BD		NM	BD		NM	BD		NM	BD
1825-1964	TP	.31	**.46	TP	.18	.22	TP	**.49	*.33	TP	**.53	*.43
	UP	.22	*.34	UP	.10	.18	UP	*.39	.26	UP	*.37	.27
	MP	*.37	**.45	MP	.12	.10	MP	*.39	.25	MP	*.39	.28
	IS	.00	.05	IS	.01	.08	IS	.23	.12	IS	**.53	*.42
1825-1944	TP	.32	**.50	TP	.27	.32	TP	*.42	*.41	TP	**.67	**.56
	UP	.16	*.38	UP	.20	.29	UP	.35	.33	UP	*.45	*.36
	MP	*.37	**.53	MP	.27	.24	MP	.33	.33	MP	**.55	*.40
	IS	−.01	.07	IS	.07	.13	IS	.19	.15	IS	**.54	*.47
1825-1919	TP	.16	.28	TP	.25	.24	TP	.37	.38	TP	**.63	.36
	UP	−.13	.05	UP	.02	.15	UP	.19	.16	UP	.34	.14
	MP	.31	.37	MP	.23	.12	MP	.24	.12	MP	*.53	.15
	IS	−.28	−.29	IS	−.17	−.23	IS	−.26	−.32	IS	.12	−.02
1850-1864	TP	.30	*.47	TP	.15	.21	TP	**.52	.33	TP	**.52	*.43
	UP	.31	*.42	UP	.16	.24	UP	**.52	.34	UP	*.49	*.38
	MP	*.39	*.47	MP	.04	.07	MP	*.40	.25	MP	.36	.29
	MX	.28	*.37	MX	.27	.32	MX	**.55	*.46	MX	*.43	.33
	IS	.07	.10	IS	.04	.13	IS	.36	.19	IS	**.63	**.53

Key to Table 4-1

1) *p is less than .05.

   **p is less than .01.

2) Column designations refer to the indices of the dependent variable:

   NM = Nation-months of war involvement begun.

   BD = Battle-deaths from war involvement begun.

3) Row designations refer to the indices of the independent variables. In the case of status inconsistency, all designations refer to the discrepancy *between* a given index and attributed diplomatic importance.

TP	= Total population	MX	= Military expenditures
UP	= Urban population	IS	= Iron/Steel production
MP	= Military personnel	DP	= Attributed diplomatic importance

For the 1825-1964 and 1825-1944 periods, the indices of status inconsistency based on military personnel and total population appear to show the greatest degree of association, although those based on urban population and military expenditure were equally good predictors for the 1850-1964 period. In all of these cases, status inconsistency showed a markedly stronger association with the number of battle-deaths than with the number of nation-months. On the other hand, the index based on iron and steel production was a strikingly *unsuccessful* predictor, with all four of the coefficients close to zero.

In the case of the 1825-1919 period, however, the observed association is less impressive; not only are none of the coefficients statistically significant (a result we might expect from the smaller N), but their absolute magnitudes are noticeably smaller as well, and, in the case of the relationship between the iron and steel index and war, are *negative*.

In a previous chapter it was suggested that status inconsistency might affect war only indirectly, and if this were true we might expect to see a rise in the observed strength of the relationship if the dependent variable was measured some period of time after the independent variables. But if we correlate the amount of status inconsistency in the system with the amount of war begun in the period starting five years later, this does not seem to be the case; introducing such a time lag does not strengthen the relationship. Indeed, most of the correlations are noticeably lower, with none significant at the .05 level. Moreover, many now have signs that are opposite to the predicted direction. The best that can be said is that the pattern of the correlations is much the same despite their decline in magnitude and significance. The indicators constructed with the total population index predict to war best not only for the period as a whole but for the 1825-1919 and 1825-1944 subperiods as well; that based on military expenditures is the best predictor for the 1850-1964 period.

When we examine the relationship of status inconsistency to the onset of war in the period beginning ten years later, however, the trend reverses itself; the results are generally comparable to those obtained when no lag was employed. For the period as a whole, and for all subperiods except 1825-1919, at least some of the correlations were moderately high in magnitude as well as statistically significant. Once again, the index based on total population seemed to be the best predictor except for the 1850-1964 period where status inconsistency based on military expenditures produced a slightly better association. As before, the index based on iron and steel predicted least well; in two cases, the observed relationship was even in the opposite direction to that predicted. The most noticeable difference between the no-lag and ten-year lag cases concerned the indices of the dependent variable; when a ten-year lag was employed, status inconsistency predicted more successfully to nation-months of war begun than to the battle death index, a switch from the no-lag situation.

But perhaps the most impressive findings—and some of the most striking changes—are obtained if we increase the time lag to fifteen years, and relate status inconsistency in the system to the amount of war begun in the quinquennial period starting a full decade and a half later. With this very long lag, we see not only that virtually all the correlations are large and in the predicted direction, but that their values increase markedly from those obtained when the dependent and independent variables are measured with less temporal separation. The largest correlation is a very high .67; such a relationship would occur less than once in a thousand by chance alone and accounts for no less than 45 percent of the variance in the dependent variable. In two other cases, 40 percent of the variance is explained, and in an additional eight results 25 percent or more of the variance is accounted for. Moreover, the preponderance of these relationships are statistically significant, thirteen at the .05 level and an additional eight at the .01 level. But even with a fifteen-year lag, status inconsistency appears to predict less well to war in the 1825-1919 period; only two of eight correlations are high and significant, while most of the remainder are quite low.

When shorter time lags were employed, the choice of indicator on both the independent and dependent variables exerted an important influence on the results. This remains true with a fifteen-year lag, but to a much lesser degree and with some noteworthy differences. As before, the index based on total population appears to be the best predictor. However, the military personnel index no longer holds the same position of relative importance; it is not a particularly strong predictor for the 140-year period as a whole, nor for the 1850-1964 subperiod. Only in the two early subperiods (1825-1944 and 1825-1919) does it even rank second to total population. On the other hand, the index based on iron and steel production enters into far *stronger* relationships, both relatively and absolutely, when this longer time lag is employed. Virtually without effect up to this point, this index is now as strong a predictor as the indicator based on total population for the period as a whole, and thus considerably more powerful than the other two indices. In two of the three subperiods its influence is also potent, as strong as the military personnel index in 1825-1944, and by far the strongest predictor of all in 1850-1964. By contrast, its influence appears negligible in the 1825-1919 period, leading us to the conclusion that the predictive capacity of the iron and steel status inconsistency index increases markedly over the century and a half of this study. Finally, as was the case when a ten-year lag was employed, indices of status inconsistency predicted better to nation-months of war involvement begun. But as with the differences between indices of the independent variables, the gap is not so wide with a fifteen-year lag; important differences exist only in the 1820-1919 period.

The Results: Status Mobility

Changing the predictor variable from status inconsistency to status mobility leaves us with a much weaker set of associations. Looking in Table 4-2 at the no-lag results, we find no correlations above the .05 threshold for the entire

Table 4-2
Correlations Between Status Mobility and National War Involvement Begun

Period Lag	No Lag			5 Years			10 Years			15 Years		
		NM	BD		NM	BD		NM	BD		NM	BD
	TP	−.06	.10	TP	−.20	−.09	TP	−.05	−.12	TP	.07	.02
	UP	.14	.03	UP	.04	.13	UP	.02	−.10	UP	**.47	.18
1825-1964	MP	.27	.17	MP	−.06	.04	MP	.08	−.04	MP	.16	.25
	IS	.08	.16	IS	.04	.24	IS	*.42	*.33	IS	**.67	**.50
	DP	.00	.06	DP	−.32	−.21	DP	−.13	−.13	DP	−.10	.04
	TP	−.11	.09	TP	−.23	−.07	TP	−.19	−.14	TP	.15	.04
	UP	.04	.04	UP	.07	.16	UP	.09	−.06	UP	*.45	.17
1825-1944	MP	.08	.19	MP	.04	.12	MP	.16	.01	MP	.19	.26
	IS	.08	.18	IS	.07	.28	IS	**.43	*.39	IS	**.72	**.56
	DP	−.10	.06	DP	−.29	−.19	DP	−.11	−.13	DP	−.04	.04
	TP	−.25	−.12	TP	−.20	−.02	TP	−.20	−.09	TP	−.11	−.12
	UP	−.07	−.07	UP	.09	.08	UP	.14	−.09	UP	.17	−.12
1825-1919	MP	.10	.20	MP	.22	.28	MP	.23	.01	MP	−.26	−.09
	IS	−.20	−.12	IS	−.09	.13	IS	*.47	*.50	IS	**.58	*.48
	DP	.00	.22	DP	−.25	−.11	DP	−.17	−.15	DP	−.26	−.18
	TP	.16	.34	TP	−.09	−.01	TP	.18	−.06	TP	.30	.19
	UP	.09	.00	UP	.01	.11	UP	−.01	−.13	UP	*.45	.16
1850-1964	MP	.31	.18	MP	−.11	.03	MP	.02	−.07	MP	.25	.30
	MX	.21	.08	MX	−.12	−.05	MX	.08	.06	MX	*.39	*.39
	IS	−.01	.10	IS	−.07	.20	IS	*.41	.31	IS	**.70	*.50
	DP	.21	.27	DP	−.18	−.19	DP	.04	−.03	DP	.12	.30

Key to Table 4-2

1) *p is less than .05.

   **p is less than .01.

2) Column designations refer to the indices of the dependent variable:

   NM = Nation-months of war involvement begun.

   BD = Battle-deaths from war involvement begun.

3) Row designations refer to the indices of the independent variables. In the case of status inconsistency, all designations refer to the discrepancy *between* a given index and attributed diplomatic importance.

TP	= Total population	MX	= Military expenditures
UP	= Urban population	IS	= Iron/Steel production
MP	= Military personnel	DP	= Attributed diplomatic importance

period or any of the three subperiods; as a matter of fact, ten of the forty-two are actually negative, contrary to our prediction. The strongest relationships are found with the military personnel index for the full 140 years and in the truncated period beginning in 1850. Also discernible are the correlations between war and mobility on total population, military expenditures, and diplomatic importance for this latter period.

If we introduce a five-year time lag, however, even this weak evidence disappears; there would seem to be virtually no positive association between the independent and the dependent variables. Indeed, the strongest and most consistent finding is the existence of a slight *negative* relationship between status mobility and war, which appears in partial contrast to the usually vanishing or positive correlations that appear with no lag. In other words, the results obtained with only a short lag would appear directly *contrary* to the second hypothesis in the study.

However, this quite negative finding is strikingly reversed when the time lag is extended to ten years. Although with most of the indices we obtain the usually vanishing, always insignificant correlations noted above, if we measure status mobility with reference to iron and steel production we uncover a fairly strong positive relationship which stands out regardless of the time period examined. All but one of the correlations so obtained are significant at the .05 level, and one would have occurred by chance less than one time in a hundred. At least with regard to industrial capability, then, there would appear to be some strong evidence confirming the second hypothesis.

This evidence is even more impressive when we look at the results obtained when the dependent variable is measured fifteen years after the independent variable. We saw that the use of such a lag increases the association between status inconsistency and war, and the same would appear to be true for the status mobility-war relationship. For all but the 1825-1919 period, the index based on urban population shows a strong relationship to war, as does that based on military expenditure for the 1850-1964 period. Once again, differential capability change based on iron and steel shows the strongest relationship to war, its magnitude being large for all time periods and greater than in the ten-year lag case. We observe correlations as high as .72, which relationship explains 52 percent of the variance in the dependent variable and would occur by chance only three times in ten thousand.

However, indices based on military personnel and total population—which attributes, as we saw, were good predictors when used to generate indices of status *inconsistency*—show as little relationship to war as they did when shorter lags were used. Equally unaffected were the results produced by differential rates of change in attributed status—just as with shorter time lags, the fifteen-year lag yielded findings very weak in magnitude and inconclusive in direction. Thus, in contrast to the status inconsistency case, the augmentation in the status mobility-war relationship produced by increased lagging is quite index-specific.

Summary

On the face of it, the bivariate correlations between our indicators would seem to offer a good deal of support for both our hypotheses. In the case of status inconsistency, the remarkable constancy in the general trend of the results over a number of different combinations of indicators, lags, and time periods, combined with the very high magnitude of some of the individual correlations, might well lead us to infer that an important factor in the genesis of international war had been identified. With regard to status mobility, although the findings are scarcely as uniform, the large magnitude of some of the correlations makes it tempting to conclude that differential rates of change in capability—at least when defined in terms of industrial production—have an important influence on war as well.

However, if these findings lend support to our hypotheses they also would seem to define important limiting and optimal conditions as well. First, in both cases, the relationships appear to be maximized if a very long time-lag is employed, with this tendency being more pronounced in the status mobility case. Second, in both cases the relationships are only significant if particular indices of the independent variables are employed, this again being more pronounced with status mobility. Finally, in both cases the relationships vary somewhat with the particular time period chosen for consideration, although this is much more visible in the case of status inconsistency.

The question now becomes, to what extent are these findings supported by further analysis? It is this question that we now seek to answer by means of stepwise multiple regression.

Multiple Regression Analysis

The Regression Model

In addition to determining the bivariate relationships between the various indicators of the independent variables and war, it is also important to examine their joint effects. It is quite conceivable that different sorts of status are salient in different conflict situations, or that mobility may produce war in different ways than by increasing status inconsistency. If so, the explanatory power of several indices taken together will be greater than that of any single index. To obtain the fullest explanatory payoff, we must determine which of the many possible combinations of indicators maximize the amount of variance accounted for in the dependent variable. This is done by employing stepwise multiple regression (Alker, 1966, pp. 17-19).[2]

The rationale behind the use of this technique is as follows. If we are attempting to predict to variable Y from a set of independent variables X_1,

$X_2 \ldots X_k$, the simplest way to explain the maximum amount of variance in Y would be to construct an equation (using the principle of least squares) in which the dependent variable Y was written as a function of *all* the predictor variables.

$$Y = a + b_1 X_1 + b_2 X_2 + \ldots b_k X_k + u \tag{4.1}$$

where a is the intercept or constant term, $b_1, b_2 \ldots b_k$ are the regression coefficients (or the amount of change in $X_1, X_2 \ldots X_k$ required to produce a unit change in Y holding all other variables constant), and u is the "error" or residual term (standing for that portion of the variation in Y not explained).

But such a procedure would scarcely yield the most parsimonious result. Since the predictor variables will almost always be interrelated, it is usually possible to substitute for the set of k variables a smaller number which account for almost as much variance. In other words, if we control for the other predictor variable, some of the X's will be found to have little influence on Y; in terms of Equation 4.1, a number of the b's will be very small, allowing us to eliminate the corresponding terms without markedly increasing u. The problem, then, is to select an optimal subset of the k possible predictor variables. This involves two tasks: first, determining the relative importance of each of the X variables as predictors to Y; and, second, deciding at what point the incremental influence of additional predictor variables are sufficiently unimportant to justify their exclusion.

In stepwise regression the first task is performed, as the name implies, in an iterative manner (Alker, 1966, pp. 17-19).[3] A two-variable equation is first constructed using the independent variable which accounts for the greatest percentage of the variance. This equation is then enlarged to three variables by including the independent variable which accounts for the most additional variance when added to the existing equation. This procedure is then repeated until either a) all of the independent variables have been included, or b) some predetermined threshold has been reached.

The second task—that of determining this threshold—is performed by measuring the statistical significance (F-probability) of the equations that are produced. That is to say, we wish to add to the equations only those explanatory variables whose effects are statistically distinguishable from random fluctuations. If they are not—whether it be because a possible predictor does not exhibit a strong bivariate relationship with the dependent variable, or because, having controlled for the *other* independent variables, its influence is negligible—then the degree of confidence we can attach to the equation so formed will be lowered. For purposes of the present study, it was decided to cease entering variables if such further additions would lower the F-probability of the resulting equation below the .05 level.

While this threshold insures that the reported results will have a low probability of being produced by chance alone, it does not guarantee their reliability. Applying the principle that additional inferences about one's data require additional assumptions, we might expect that in moving from bivariate to multivariate analysis, still more conditions must be fulfilled. Such indeed is the case (Johnston, 1963, pp. 106-8). Most of these requirements need not concern us here, but two raise important problems in this study and therefore merit detailed attention.

First, when we attempt to discover the joint effect of several variables, it is important that they themselves not be *too* highly intercorrelated (Johnston, 1963, Chapter 8-1; Blalock, 1962, pp. 87-90; Forbes and Tufte, 1968). If they are, a pathological situation known as multicollinearity develops in the equation making it difficult or impossible to distinguish between the effects of the separate variables. In the limiting case where the intercorrelations between the independent variables approach unity, their effects are not distinguishable at all, with any observed differences between the coefficients being entirely due to error variance. Thus, in the case of stepwise regression, the decision as to which of two highly intercorrelated variables to include in the equation may be based on very small differences in the coefficients, and, consequently, will be very sensitive to error. Since our intuitive beliefs about the indices of our independent variables would lead us to predict strong interrelationships, it is important to exercise care in the interpretation of the results. In particular, it would be wise to avoid making too much of decisions to include or exclude a specific index from an equation when it is highly correlated with some other independent variable.

A second difficulty inheres in the use of the regression model in time-series analysis, and is much less easy to detect than multicollinearity: serially correlated residual terms. Basic to the regression model is the assumption that the residuals (the differences between the actual values of the data points and their values as estimated by the regression equation) are not related to one another (Johnston, 1963, Chapter 7; Christ, 1966, Chapter 10-4). In our case, this assumption is equivalent to saying there is no sequential relationship between the values of the residuals at t_0, t_1, t_2 etc. But suppose—as is not unlikely—some important independent variables have been omitted from the equation, with the result that the error term accounts for a good percentage of the variance in the dependent variable. Then if, as in the present case, there is *some* autocorrelation in the dependent variable (Singer and Small, 1970, Chapter 9), this will almost certainly be reflected in the error term. If this assumption of the regression model is violated, the least-squares method of estimating the regression line may both *overestimate* the amount of variance accounted for by the predictor variables and *underestimate* the probability that the results ever be produced by chance alone, especially when time lags are employed. In other words, autocorrelated residuals can make our results seem considerably better than they are in fact.

At the present early stage in the development of quantitative international politics, it would be difficult to justify undertaking elaborate procedures to correct for autocorrelation when there are so many other factors which may bias the result. But it is certainly worthwhile to determine the extent to which serial relationships do exist amongst the residuals of our equations, so that due care may be taken in their interpretation. Thus, the Durbin-Watson test for autocorrelated residuals will be employed, and the results reported with the equations.

Let us now look at the results themselves. In what ways do the regression equations confirm, and to what extent do they disconfirm, the bivariate findings?

Results

There are a number of different ways in which we might group the indices for purposes of multiple regression analysis. Three procedures shall be employed. First, we shall treat status inconsistency and status mobility *separately*, and attempt to construct equations which predict to the amount of war begun using first the five indices of status inconsistency, and then the six indices of status mobility. This procedure allows us to compare the predictive capacity of each of the two independent variables on the basis of the total amount of variance explained by *all* its indices rather than comparing them index by index.

Second, we shall examine the joint effects of the two independent variables, using one index at a time. Here we group together each index of status inconsistency with that index of status mobility computed with reference to the same dimension of capability. This enables us to obtain five different measures of the combined effects of the two variables. At the same time, it permits us to compare the relative utility of the various indices of national capability, taking into account the combined influence of the indices of inconsistency and mobility based upon them.

Finally, we shall examine the joint effects of all indices of both independent variables, in order to determine the maximum amount of variance in the two indices of our independent variable which can be explained using the data in this study to its fullest advantage. The equations resulting from these three operations are displayed together in Table 4-3.

Turning first to the combined effects of the several indices of status inconsistency, we find that the proportion of variance explained often exceeds that accounted for by any single index by a substantial margin. Combined by stepwise regression procedures, these various indices explain from about one-third to about one-half of the variance in nation-months and battle-deaths of war. As in the case of the bivariate analysis, the results show notable variations with the time period and lag chosen. First, as a general rule, the greater the lag, the greater the proportion of variance explained; with no lag, this figure hovers around 30 percent, and moves upward fairly steadily to reach a maximum of

Table 4-3

Stepwise Regression Equations Predicting from Status Mobility and Status Inconsistency to National War Involvement Begun

Period	Time Lag in Years	Dependent Variable Index	Independent Variable Indices Entered (See key)	Multiple R^2	F-level (P)	Durbin-Watson (d)
1825-1964	0	Battle-deaths	INCPOP, INCPER, INCSTL	30.0	.039	.88 (p=.01)
			INCPOP, INCSTL, MOBSTL	31.6	.030	.80 (p=.01)
	10	Nation-months	MOBURB, MOBSTL	24.3	.046	2.10
			INCPOP, MOBPOP, MOBURB, MOBSTL	37.9	.041	2.27
	15	Nation-months	MOBURB, MOBSTL	46.9	.001	2.35
			INCPOP, INCURB, INCPER, INCSTL	43.5	.023	2.06
			INCSTL, MOBPOP, MOBSTL	55.5	.0009	2.45
			INCSTL, MOBSTL, MOBDIP	53.2	.0015	2.24
		Battle-deaths	MOBURB, MOBSTL	25.5	.012	2.07
			INCSTL, MOBPOP, MOBURB, MOBSTL, MOBDIP	43.8	.048	.76 (p=.025)
1825-1944	0	Battle-deaths	INCPOP, INCPER, INCSTL	35.4	.030	.92 (p=.025)
	10	Nation-months	INCPOP, INCSTL, MOBSTL	33.7	.038	1.22
			MOBPOP, MOBSTL	27.3	.048	1.76
	15	Nation-months	INCPOP, MOBPOP, MOBDIP	47.6	.010	1.81
			INCSTL, MOBSTL, MOBDIP	62.1	.0008	2.17
1825-1944	15	Nation-months	INCPOP, INCURB, INCSTL	54.4	.003	1.54
			INCPER, INCSTL, MOBSTL	66.7	.0003	2.06

Year		Dependent	Independent Variables			
		Battle-deaths	INCPOP, INCURB, INCSTL	30.3	.033	1.43
1825-1919	0		INCPOP, INCURB, INCSTL, MOBPOP, MOBURB, MOBSTL, MOBDIP	63.8	.031	.91
		Nation-months	INCPOP, INCURB, INCPER, MOBPOP, MOBDIP	56.6	.035	2.29
	10	Battle-deaths	INCPOP, INCURB, INCPER, MOBPOP, MOBDIP	64.7	.011	2.17
		Nation-months	INCPOP, INCSTL	35.8	.044	2.01
			MOBPOP, MOBSTL	27.3	.048	1.76
	15	Battle-deaths	INCPOP, INCSTL	43.8	.018	2.43
			INCPOP, INCSTL, MOBSTL	47.7	.033	2.44
		Nation-months	INCPOP, MOBPOP, MOBDIP	50.2	.034	2.37
			MOBPER, MOBSTL	38.2	.043	1.91
			INCPER, INCSTL, MOBPER, MOBSTL	59.1	.031	1.53
1850-1964	0	Battle-deaths	INCPER, INCSTL	27.2	.048	1.67
		Nation-months	INCPOP, MOBPOP, MOBEXP, MOBSTL	41.4	.048	1.43
	5		INCPOP, INCPER, INCEXP, INCSTL	44.4	0.43	2.11
		Battle-deaths	INCPOP, INCURB, INCPER, INCEXP, MOBPOP, MOBEXP, MOBSTL	71.3	.009	2.70
			INCPER, INCEXP, INCSTL	48.9	.008	2.28
			INCURB, INCPER, INCEXP, INCSTL, MOBPOP, MOBSTL	56.7	.040	1.33
1850-1964	10	Nation-months	INCURB, MOBURB, MOBDIP	40.7	.035	2.10
			INCEXP, MOBEXP, MOBDIP	38.1	.048	2.40
			INCPOP, INCPER, INCEXP	42.8	.027	2.80
		Battle-deaths	INCURB, INCPER, INCEXP, MOBPOP, MOBURB, MOBPER	61.6	.028	2.17
			INCPER, INCEXP, INCSTL	42.9	.026	2.44
			INCPER, INCEXP, MOBURB, MOBPER, MOBSTL	58.8	.019	2.78

Table 4-3 (cont.)

Period	Time Lag in Years	Dependent Variable Index	Independent Variable Indices Entered (See key)	Multiple R^2	F-level (P)	Durbin-Watson (d)
	15	Nation-months	INCSTL, MOBSTL, MOBDIP	53.5	.008	2.18
			INCSTL, MOBSTL, MOBDIP	57.4	.004	2.28
			MOBPOP, MOBURB, MOBPER, MOBEXP, MOBSTL	68.4	.006	1.38
		Battle-deaths	INCSTL, MOBSTL, MOBDIP	57.4	.004	2.28
			MOBPOP, MOBEXP, MOBSTL	42.9	.034	1.86

Key to Table 4-3

1) Index designations:

INC	= Status inconsistency	PER	= Military personnel
MOB	= Status mobility	EXP	= Military expenditures
POP	= Total population	STL	= Iron/Steel production
URB	= Urban population	DIP	= Diplomatic importance

2) Where the value of the Durbin-Watson statistic (d) gives conclusive evidence of serially-correlated residuals, the statistical significance of this finding is entered.

over 50 percent with a fifteen-year lag. Second, in general more variance is explained if we attempt to predict to war within a *subperiod* of our temporal domain rather than the 140-year period as a whole. The maximum R^2 for the 1825-1964 period is .435; this is exceeded in all subperiods, being .502 for 1825-1919, .535 for 1850-1964, and .544 for 1825-1944. On the other hand, we observe no clear-cut patterns regarding particular indices of the independent variables; they appear to be almost equally prevalent in the equations. The same appears to be true for the dependent variables; although significant equations cannot be constructed to predict to both indices for some time periods and lags, neither index seems to be noticeably favored considering the results as a whole.

A rather different picture emerges if we enter only the different indices of status mobility into the equation. Here a substantial additional predictive capacity is obtained only when the largest possible time-lag is employed. With no lag or a five-year lag, not a single significant equation could be constructed, and with a ten-year lag only 24.3 percent of the variance can be explained; however, when the lag is extended to fifteen years this rises to a maximum of 68.4 percent. Nor are the results uniform with respect to the time period examined. No significant equations can be constructed for the 1825-1919 and 1825-1944 periods, but good results are obtained for the 140 years as a whole, (25.5 percent of the variance explained in battle-deaths begun, and 46.9 percent in nation-months begun), and these are even better for the 1850-1964 subperiod (47.9 percent and 68.4 percent of the variance explained in battle-deaths and nation-months respectively), indicating that the effect of status mobility appears to have increased with the passage of time. Finally, there is a very noticeable difference between indicators in these results; the index based on iron and steel *always* appears while the index of diplomatic status does not enter any of the equations.

Although these results would seem very favorable to both our hypotheses, a note of caution should be injected at this point. The table shows that the residuals from several of the equations when no time lag was employed show significant evidence of autocorrelation, which, as noted in the previous chapter, implies that the estimates of error variance may be biased. Since this result only occurred in a very few equations it was not deemed necessary to employ alternate procedures of estimation, but it should be noted that in those equations affected the least squares procedures may have overestimated the R^2 and underestimated the probability that the results could have occurred by chance alone (Johnston, 1963, Chapter 7). Since these equations are at any rate amongst the weakest, with R^2 values in the .30 range, it is doubtful that they represent evidence of a significant relationship.

If grouping the indices of status inconsistency and status mobility *separately* increases our ability to explain the magnitude and severity of war, a similar result should occur when we *combine* the effects of these two variables. And, indeed, if we examine the joint impact of the two variables using in each case the same index of national capability, we find again that to some extent our predictive capacity has been improved. In some cases, we can now account for about half of the variance in the dependent variable, and in one instance this proportion rises to almost two-thirds. However, these results are by no means consistent. First, only when a substantial time lag is introduced do we observe effects which have a significant probability of being due to more than chance variation. As we can see from the table, no significant equations are generated in this way when no lag is employed or with a five-year lag, and the number rises to six with a fifteen-year lag. Second, not all indices are equally good predictors; the indices based on iron and steel production seem to explain more of the variance than those based on total population, urban population, or military expenditures, and the index based on military personnel—contrary to what one might expect from examining the bivariate correlations—nowhere enters an equation. Finally, there is some variation between the various time-periods. The largest R^2 with a ten-year lag is obtained for the 1850-1964 subperiod, with no significant equation generated for the 1825-1919 and 1825-1944 periods; with a fifteen-year lag, the largest R^2 is found for the 1825-1944 period, with significant equations being generated for all segments of the temporal domain.

Since the use of status inconsistency and mobility based on the same index increases the amount of variance explained, and since much the same effect takes place when we enter simultaneously different indices of our variables considered separately, then we might expect that if we allowed all indices of all the independent variables to enter the equations, our predictive capacity would be still further enhanced. Such indeed appears to be the case, although this step seems to have been more successful in increasing the number and variety of significant equations than in augmenting further the maximum R^2. In all of the subperiods under examination, combinations of indicators could be discovered which explained about two-thirds of the variance in at least one indicator of thy dependent variable, and for the period as a whole approximately half of the variance in both indices could be accounted for.

Even more striking, perhaps, than the magnitude of this relationship is its remarkable consistency when compared to the results reported above; there seems to be relatively little relationship between the amount of variance explained and the particular time-lag employed. Indeed, the five-year time-lag, which produced the *least* satisfactory results in all analyses examined thus far, now yields the largest percentage of variance explained: 71.3 percent. The only thing which detracts from this generally bright picture is the discovery, once again, of serially correlated residuals. Although these are scarcely widespread enough to affect our impressions of the findings as a whole, the danger of producing biased results under these conditions is so great (Johnston, 1963, pp. 215-6; Christ, 1966, Chapter 9-13) that considerable caution should be used in interpreting these R^2 values.

At any rate, it would seem that the evidence obtained by multiple regression analysis confirms and strengthens the impression obtained from the bivariate correlations; both status inconsistency and mobility are closely associated with the onset of war in the international system. The regression results suggest further that the two status based variables act even more powerfully in combination, almost strikingly so; in every case they were together able to explain a substantial proportion and often a preponderance of the variance in international war.

But whatever multiple regression may tell us about the *joint* effect of our variables, it cannot give us the answers to two vital questions. First, it will not enable us to tell if the variables are genuinely independent, or whether, as was suggested, the status inconsistency-war relationship is not merely an artifact of an underlying relationship between status mobility and war. Second, it will not enable us to determine if status mobility has a *direct* influence on war, or alternatively if it is only an *indirect* cause, operating by stimulating changes in the level of status inconsistency in the system (Alker, 1966, p. 18). Since both variables were entered into the regression equations described above, and since in some cases there is a good deal of intercorrelation between indices of status inconsistency and status mobility, it is not possible to give definitive answers to these questions without using a different technique.

Dependence Analysis

The Dependence Equations

Among the methods for inferring a causal network amongst variables, the one most appropriate for present purposes is known as dependence analysis. Developed by Raymond Boudon (1968), it is essentially an extension of the path analysis techniques associated with Sewell Wright (1934). Its purpose is to decompose bivariate correlation coefficients into dependence coefficients (Wright's path coefficients), another name for the standardized partial regression coefficients of all independent variables on each dependent variable. Just as the unstandardized regression coefficients may be interpreted as the amount of change in the dependent or outcome variable produced by a unit change in the independent or predictor variable, so the standardized regression coefficients may be interpreted as the amount of change so produced when the variables are standardized. In other words, they are "the fraction of the standard deviation of the dependent variable ... for which the designated factors are responsible," (Wright, 1934, p. 162) holding constant all other variables in the model. This technique offers three advantages over the Simon and Blalock methods of causal modelling.

First, it allows us to determine precisely the direct effect of each independent variable on the current dependent variable. This makes it possible not only to detect spurious relationships, but also to determine the relative importance of the several independent variables. Second, where there are indirect as well as direct causal connections between variables, dependence analysis allows us to determine the relative importance of each "causal" pathway. A final advantage is that it allows us to depart somewhat from normal causal modelling usage in that we need make no assumptions as to which independent variables do, and which do not, affect the variables below them in the causal hierarchy. As Choucri and North (1969, p. 42) point out, such a procedure is permissible using dependence analysis, and is more suited to the present explanatory state of the present study than the testing of specific predictive models.

Now, based on the earlier theoretical discussion, we can write, in normal regression form:

$$X_2 = b_{12}X_1 + u_2 \qquad (4.2)$$

$$X_3 = b_{13}X_1 + b_{23}X_2 + u_3 \qquad (4.3)$$

$$X_4 = b_{14}X_1 + b_{24}X_2 + b_{34}X_3 + u_4 \qquad (4.4)$$

where X_1 is differential change in capability in the system, X_2 is differential change in diplomatic status, X_3 is the level of system-wide status inconsistency, X_4 represents the amount of international war begun in the system, and where the b's are the unstandardized regression coefficients, and the u's the variation in each dependent variable unaccounted for by the current predictor variables. (The variables are assumed to have zero means in order to remove the intercept term.) Boudon (1968) has shown that if we substitute the standardized regression coefficients (β) by dividing through by the ratio of the appropriate standard deviations, we can transform each of the foregoing equations into a linear system in which we can solve for the β's in terms of the empirical correlation coefficients (r's). Let us illustrate this with reference to Equation 4.3. Substituting standardized coefficients, we obtain

$$X_3 = \beta_{13}(\sigma_3/\sigma_1)X_1 + \beta_{23}(\sigma_3/\sigma_2)X_2 + u_3. \qquad (4.5)$$

Multiplying by X_1,

$$X_3X_1 = \beta_{13}(\sigma_3/\sigma_1)X_1^2 + \beta_{23}(\sigma_3/\sigma_2)X_2X_1 + u_3X_1. \qquad (4.6)$$

Now from the standard score form for the correlation coefficient

$$r_{xy} = \Sigma \, xy/N\sigma_x\sigma_y$$

we can write

$$\Sigma \, xy = Nr_{xy} \, \sigma_x\sigma_y.$$

Thus the mathematical *expectation* or predicted value for any $x_i y_i$ (assuming normally distributed variables) is equal to $r_{xy}\sigma_x\sigma_y$. This equality enables us to substitute correlation coefficients and standard deviations for the cross-product terms in Equation 4.5, viz.:

$$r_{13}\sigma_3\sigma_1 = \beta_{13}(\sigma_3/\sigma_1)\sigma_1{}^2 + \beta_{23}(\sigma_1/\sigma_2)\ r_{12}\sigma_1\sigma_2 + r_{u1}\sigma_1\sigma_u. \quad (4.7)$$

If we assume that the error term is not correlated with any of the independent variables, r_{u2} equals zero, and Equation 4.7 reduces to

$$\beta_{13} + \beta_{23}r_{12} = r_{13}. \quad (4.8)$$

Similarly, multiplying 4.5 by X_2, we would obtain

$$\beta_{13}r_{12} + \beta_{23} = r_{23}. \quad (4.9)$$

It is obvious that we can solve 4.8 and 4.9 for β_{13} and β_{23} in terms of r_{12}, r_{13} and r_{23}. Performing the same steps on Equation 4.3, we obtain

$$\beta_{14} + \beta_{24}r_{12} + \beta_{34}r_{13} = r_{14} \quad (4.10)$$

$$\beta_{14}r_{12} + \beta_{24} + \beta_{34}r_{23} = r_{24} \quad (4.11)$$

$$\beta_{14}r_{13} + \beta_{24}r_{23} + \beta_{34} = r_{34} \quad (4.12)$$

allowing us to solve for all dependence coefficients.

Note that in deriving the previous equations, two crucial assumptions were made: that the variables were distributed normally and that the error term was independent of the other predictor variables. The first assumption has already been dealt with, and we saw that at least in the bivariate case no serious distortions were created by the fact that our data depart somewhat from normality. This finding indicates that this assumption is unproblematic as regards dependence analysis.

A more serious difficulty is posed by the need to assume an independent error term, i.e., that there are no other variables not specified in the model which act directly on both the dependent variable and one or more of the predictor variables at once. Since data-based studies about the origins of international war are still few and far between no research design can confidently exclude such a possibility. If the error term is not in fact independent, the values of the dependence coefficients computed from Equations 4.8-4.12 may be serious *overestimates* of their true values. For example, if in Equation 4.11 $_{u2} \neq 0$, then 4.8 becomes

$$\beta_{13} + \beta_{23}r_{12} + r_{u2}\sigma_2\sigma_u/\sigma_1\sigma_2 = r_{13} \quad (4.13)$$

and with the presence of the additional term on the left hand side it is obvious that the values of β_{13} and β_{23} will be reduced. After presenting the results we shall explore some possible conditions under which the error term might not be independent, but for the moment it is sufficient to note that dependence coefficients, no less than bivariate correlations, depend not only upon the calculations made from the data but also upon the theoretical assumptions which govern our choice of variables.

The Results

Beginning with those cases in which no time lag is employed, a fairly clear pattern seems to emerge, as we see at a glance from Table 4-4. In general, status inconsistency appears to have the predicted effect on war, even holding constant mobility on both the capability and reputational dimensions. The standardized partial regression coefficients of status inconsistency on war are nearly all positive in direction and moderate to strong in magnitude. On the other hand, status mobility does *not* seem to have a strong direct effect on war; holding status inconsistency constant, the relationship appears to vanish in most cases. Rather, it would appear to affect war indirectly through status inconsistency. Mobility on the capability dimensions of status—and, sometimes, on the reputational dimension as well—appears to have a strong positive influence on status inconsistency, thus indicating the presence of an important two-step link between these independent variables and the indices of our dependent variable.

However, these generalizations do not hold for all indices and all time periods. For one thing, the results in the 1825-1919 period do not conform to the general pattern; when we use total population and military personnel as capability indices, status mobility would appear to have a strong *negative* relationship to war, whereas reputational status mobility and status inconsistency are positively related. Using other indices, status inconsistency predicts scarcely at all to war, and status mobility only slightly. Second, regardless of the time period used, if iron and steel production is chosen as the index of capability, virtually no positive results whatever are obtained; neither status inconsistency nor status mobility predicts to war in any important fashion here.

The same general pattern appears to prevail when we look at the results using five-year lags. Once again, status inconsistency predicts to war *directly*, and status mobility *indirectly* via status inconsistency, for all indices except those based on iron and steel production; in this case, neither variable has a strong effect on the magnitude and severity of war. The 1825-1919 period remains as before something of an exception with only the index of inconsistency based on total population showing a discernible relationship with war. However, as we might expect from the bivariate results, the relationships uncovered using a five-year lag are by no means as strong. Status inconsistency no longer appears to be so satisfactory a predictor, as virtually all the coefficients are lower than their counterparts in the zero-lag situation. Moreover, the role of status mobility as a predictor has declined to virtually nil, the signs of the coefficients often being negative and their magnitude weak. However, status mobility, both on the capability and reputational dimensions, continues to predict quite strongly to status inconsistency.

If the general trend of the results is somewhat blurred when the correlations calculated on the basis of a five-year lag are substituted in the equations, the picture comes into much sharper focus when we shift to a ten-year lag. Once again, we observe that the chief *direct* effect on war is produced by status inconsistency, and this result holds here regardless of which time-period we examine. Furthermore, the relationship would appear to be quite strong, explaining as much as 62 percent of the variance in our nation-months index, and up to 41 percent in the number of battle-deaths from war begun. But when the iron and steel capability index is employed, the result obtained is in marked contrast to this pattern and unlike any of the results produced with zero and five-year lags. Status *mobility* is now the best predictor to the amount of war begun and status inconsistency—holding status mobility constant—has much less effect. As with the other indices, though, status mobility appears to predict well to inconsistency, explaining as much as 31 percent of the variance. Thus, in contrast to the other indices (in which the results indicate an *indirect* relationship between status mobility and war via status inconsistency), the findings here would suggest a *direct* mobility-war relationship, with the relationship between status inconsistency and war being partly or wholly spurious.

The results obtained by using a fifteen-year lag follow this pattern quite closely in general direction. Interestingly enough, however, they do not continue the general upward trend in magnitude of relationship that we observe with increasing lags both in the bivariate correlations and the multiple regressions. For the 140-year period as a whole, the overall magnitude of the relationships is about the same, even declining somewhat if we examine the 1850-1964 subperiod. Only if we take the subperiods based on the earlier part of the temporal domain do we see a continuing increase; there is a slight rise for the 1825-1944 period, and a rather more substantial one in the smaller 1825-1919 time segment.

Apart from this, the results obtained using a fifteen-year lag are similar to those found with a ten-year lag; once again, if iron and steel production is employed as an index of capability, status mobility becomes a more significant factor than inconsistency, and as before mobility predicts well to inconsistency.

The Findings and the Hypotheses

Having outlined the empirical findings in detail, it remains to set forth the major patterns and trends and relate them to our hypotheses; to what extent, and under what conditions, do these appear to be confirmed or disconfirmed?

Table 4-4
Dependence Coefficients for Status Mobility and Status Inconsistency on War, and Status Mobility on Status Inconsistency

Lag (in years)	Index of Capability Status	β_{14}		β_{24}		1825-1964 β_{34}		β_{13}	β_{23}
		NM	BD	NM	BD	NM	BD		
0	TP	-.20	-.06	.06	.04	.36	.48	.33	-.06
	UP	.06	-.12	-.08	-.05	.22	.41	.37	.26
	MP	.14	-.07	-.05	.07	.30	.48	.50	-.10
	IS	.10	.18	.01	.07	-.04	-.04	.43	.18
5	TP	-.12	-.04	-.28	-.22	.26	.25	.35	-.08
	UP	.01	.07	-.38	-.29	.21	.24	.35	.27
	MP	-.05	.07	-.31	-.23	.14	.07	.49	-.10
	IS	.00	.22	-.32	-.20	.05	-.02	.44	.19
10	TP	-.18	-.22	-.09	-.05	.56	.41	.39	-.11
	UP	-.17	-.24	-.27	-.22	.55	.42	.38	.25
	MP	-.08	-.16	-.11	-.09	.42	.32	.48	-.12
	IS	.38	.33	-.12	-.11	-.08	-.01	.44	.17
15	TP	-.22	-.21	-.14	.12	.55	.48	.42	-.17
	UP	.10	.39	-.03	-.21	.24	.28	.33	.23
	MP	.05	.17	-.08	-.03	.37	.22	.37	-.14
	IS	.53	.41	-.09	-.05	.32	.24	.44	.17

		1825-1944							
0	TP	-.24	-.14	.01	.10	.39	.54	.42	-.17
	UP	-.02	-.11	-.16	-.04	.21	.43	.33	.23
	MP	-.05	-.02	-.10	.11	.14	.54	.37	-.14
	IS	.08	.20	-.09	.08	-.03	-.03	.44	.17
5	TP	-.19	-.34	-.20	-.21	.34	.35	.31	-.09
	UP	-.02	-.04	-.38	-.30	.31	.37	.36	.26
	MP	.01	.09	-.27	-.20	.25	.19	.35	-.15
	IS	.00	.24	-.30	-.18	.11	.06	.42	.17
10	TP	-.36	-.23	-.04	-.05	.51	.47	.30	-.05
	UP	-.04	-.20	-.25	-.26	.44	.49	.32	.29
	MP	.09	-.09	-.11	-.09	.29	.35	.34	-.13
	IS	.40	.37	-.09	-.11	.06	.03	.37	.19
15	TP	.08	-.16	-.20	.04	.68	.60	.31	-.03
	UP	.33	.05	-.23	-.11	.41	.38	.33	.32
	MP	.03	.13	-.02	-.03	.55	.36	.36	-.11
	IS	.59	.46	-.08	.00	.37	.31	.36	.21

Table 4-4 (cont.)

1825-1919

Lag (in years)	Index of Capability Status	β_{14}		β_{24}		β_{34}		β_{13}	β_{23}
		NM	BD	NM	BD	NM	BD		
0	TP	-.46	-.50	.27	.51	.23	.35	.25	-.09
	UP	-.04	-.07	.04	.22	-.13	.00	.28	.32
	MP	.05	-.50	.04	.51	.31	.35	.25	-.09
	IS	-.20	-.06	-.01	.24	-.27	-.31	.03	.10
5	TP	-.14	.03	-.20	-.15	.30	.24	.21	-.03
	UP	.06	.19	-.29	-.17	.10	.20	.30	.33
	MP	.24	.29	-.26	-.13	.19	.09	.07	-.13
	IS	-.15	.12	-.28	-.17	-.16	-.23	.02	.07
10	TP	-.32	-.14	.02	-.06	.44	.42	.38	-.23
	UP	.06	-.18	-.25	-.24	.25	.28	.30	.32
	MP	.24	.02	-.15	-.13	.21	.09	.00	-.24
	IS	.45	.49	-.06	-.01	-.24	-.30	.00	.14
15	TP	-.12	-.15	-.22	-.01	.68	.40	.36	-.19
	UP	.36	-.21	-.42	-.27	.47	.30	.29	.34
	MP	-.22	-.07	-.12	-.14	.49	.11	-.19	-.23
	IS	.55	.47	-.18	-.09	.13	-.02	.03	.13

			1850-1964					
0	TP	-.04	.09	.09	.06	.29	.38	.48	.26
	UP	-.08	-.27	.08	.12	.31	.49	.39	.36
	MP	.22	-.23	-.15	.15	.35	.53	.36	.30
	MX	.05	-.25	.08	.19	.22	.43	.44	.27
	IS	-.13	.04	.22	.27	.07	.01	.50	.14
5	TP	-.23	-.141	-.28	-.32	.41	.43	.50	.25
	UP	-.07	.01	-.33	-.38	.35	.41	.37	.36
	MP	-.02	.28	-.29	-.50	.21	.18	.36	.29
	MX	-.29	-.22	-.32	-.38	.57	.62	.42	.27
	IS	-.09	.10	-.21	.43	.16	.07	.52	.15
10	TP	-.16	-.37	-.18	-.14	.69	.62	.52	.21
	UP	-.37	-.40	-.19	-.18	.79	.63	.43	.30
	MP	-.24	-.27	-.09	-.07	.57	.44	.38	.25
	MX	-.20	-.16	-.18	-.24	.73	.64	.38	.27
	IS	.34	.33	-.11	-.14	.19	.04	.56	.08
15	TP	.00	-.16	-.10	.18	.56	.46	.53	.18
	UP	.29	-.02	-.10	.20	.38	.33	.41	.25
	MP	.19	.13	-.15	.14	.33	.17	.31	.23
	MX	.26	.27	-.08	.16	.34	.15	.36	.25
	IS	.54	.25	-.12	.14	.34	.35	.56	-.06

Key to Table 4-4

As per equations 4-8 to 4-12, the βs represent normalized partial regression coefficients:

β_{14} = Capability status mobility on war

β_{24} = Attributed status mobility on war

β_{34} = Status inconsistency on war

β_{13} = Capability status mobility on status inconsistency

β_{23} = Attributed status mobility on status inconsistency.

Status Inconsistency

To begin with, the findings as a whole strongly suggest that the hypothesis linking the amount of status inconsistency in the international system to the magnitude and severity of international war begun is confirmed. Whether we examine the simple bivariate correlation, measure the joint effect of the various indices by multiple regression, or hold status mobility constant via dependence analysis, we find strong and significant relationships. Moreover, we find such relationships not only for the 140-year temporal domain taken as a whole, but also for the 95 years from 1825 to 1919, the 120 years from 1825 to 1944, and the 115 years from 1850 to 1964. Despite this general finding, however, the evidence was no means completely uniform; under some conditions the hypothesis was more strongly supported than others, and quite often the differences were striking.

First, while the evidence strongly suggests confirmation of the hypothesis in the case of inconsistencies between *demographic or military* capability on the one hand, and attributed importance on the other, there is little or no confirmation in the case of inconsistencies between *industrial* capability and attributed status. Not only were the correlations and regressions in the case of the latter variable generally indicative of a much weaker relationship, but even in those instances where a strong bivariate or joint relationship *was* uncovered, the use of dependence analysis showed the relationship to be wholly or partly spurious, a result not obtained with the other indices.

Second, the evidence suggests that the most important relationship between status inconsistency and war is a long-term one. Regardless of the analytic method used, we see that a ten or fifteen-year lag produces a stronger and more significant relationship. However, the situation is not completely clear-cut; the effect of status inconsistency does not increase in a straightforward fashion with an increasing lag, and there is evidence of a moderately strong and significant relationship even with little or no lag. This may indicate, perhaps, that status inconsistency has both a short-term and a long-term influence on war.

Third, it would seem that the relationship is somewhat nonadditive with respect to time. Although the magnitudes of the correlation coefficients are roughly similar for all periods examined, multivariate analysis gives us a somewhat different picture. In general, the later the time-period, the larger the percentage of variance explained by the joint effect of the several indices, and the greater the effect of status inconsistency holding status mobility constant. These findings would seem to suggest that influence of status inconsistency on the genesis of war has *increased* over the almost century and a half under study. Moreover, not only the magnitude, but also the nature of the relationship varies with the time-period; the later the period, the greater the relative importance of inconsistencies involving the urban and industrial dimensions of capacity, and the shorter the time-lag needed to observe the maximum relationship.

Status Mobility

Turning now to the hypothesis linking differential status mobility in the international system with the amount of war begun, we find on the whole far *less* evidence that would suggest confirmation if we examine the direct relationship only. Not only are the bivariate correlations generally rather low, but there is very little evidence that the several status mobility variables jointly predict well to war, and when one controls for status inconsistency the mobility-war relationship appears to be spurious in most cases. It is either consistently low in magnitude, as in the case of mobility on the capability dimensions, or fluctuating wildly depending on the other indices used, as in the case of mobility on attributed status. Mobility on all dimensions of capability status does, however, predict strongly to status inconsistency, although mobility on attributed importance does not do so. This suggests that our second hypothesis is largely confirmed after all, but that the relationship is usually indirect. Even though we find some important deviations from the pattern, our earlier hunch is by and large borne out: status mobility appears to lead to status inconsistency which in turn predicts to war. What are the exceptions? First, when differential status mobility is measured in terms of industrial capacity, the evidence indicates our second hypothesis to be directly confirmed; not only are the bivariate relationships quite strong, but even holding status inconsistency constant, differential mobility predicts well to war. However, using any other measure of differential capability change, or differential change in attributed importance, does not yield this result. Thus, the evidence suggests that differential changes in industrial capacity are related to war in quite a different fashion than those on the other status continua examined here.

Second, our findings indicate that this direct relationship varies enormously with the period examined and the time-lag employed. The greater the lag and the later the period, the stronger the evidence of a direct relationship, suggesting that the effect is a long term one and has grown over the 140 years from Vienna to Vietnam.

Third, and in contrast to this last-mentioned result, the relationship between differential capability change and status inconsistency is much less sensitive to the time-period under examination, being approximately of the same magnitude whenever examined. This suggests in turn that the strength of the evidence for an indirect relationship between differential mobility and war varies approximately with that for the existence of a direct relationship between status inconsistency and war, following the changing patterns of this latter relationship with regard to time lags, periods, and indicators as described above.

Finally, the evidence seems to suggest a strong joint effect between mobility on certain status dimensions and inconsistency on others. Although (unlike most of the other major findings in the study) there appears to be little regularity with regard to periods, lags, and indicators, it would seem that inconsistencies between demographic capability and attributed importance generally combine with differential mobility on industrial capability to give the strongest evidence of such a joint effect. This finding suggests that, rather than being opposed, the two hypotheses of this study are in fact strongly complementary. Instead of identifying one important factor associated with the onset of war, we have evidence of the existence of two.

Notes

1. It is a common—albeit misleading—statistical usage to refer to the amount of variance "explained" by one or more predictor variables. This does not mean, of course, that we have demonstrated a causal link between the predictor and the outcome variables.

2. For general treatment of the multiple regression model, see Johnston (1963, Chapter 4) and Christ (1966, Chapter 9).

3. Despite appearances, it cannot be done merely by constructing Equation 4.1 and selecting those variables with the largest coefficients. Since the a's in the equation are partial regression coefficents (that is, they express the influence of each independent variable holding constant all others) their values will depend on which other variables are included in the final equation. Therefore we cannot base our decision concerning which variables to include on the magnitude of these coefficients, since this would result in a circular definition.

5 A Few Caveats

Introduction

In the previous chapter the results were reported and summarized. The next major step is to account for and interpret them, offering explanations for the observed patterns and trends, and assessing what they add to our knowledge of the international system. In doing so, it will often be necessary for the discussion to range "beyond the data," merging these findings with other bodies of evidence, hypotheses, and theoretical propositions. To avoid any possibility that speculation and fact will thereby be mixed, and to prevent any confusion about what is being claimed for these results, we will begin the process of interpretation in this chapter with a discussion of the *limitations* of the present study. What is it that has *not* been demonstrated, and thus what inferences would be erroneous or misleading? In other words, we shall now be concerned with the likelihood of what the statisticians refer to as Type I errors, which occur when apparent conclusions are in fact false. There would appear to be seven possible sources of such error in this study.

Reliability

To begin with, it would be a mistake to regard these results as a reliable demonstration of the existence of a statistical association between status mobility and inconsistency in the international system, and the magnitude and severity of international war begun. There are two factors which combine to make these tests less than definitive from the reliability point of view: first, despite the care with which the data were generated, there are possible sources of error and bias which may have resulted in their distortion or contamination, and, second, several features of the research design render the results particularly sensitive to such data error.

Sources of Error

The foremost reason for biased data values is, of course, inaccurate or misleading information in the sources used for the data-making operation. As outlined in Chapter 3, wherever possible information collected has been cross-checked;

nevertheless, it was sometimes necessary to rely on statistics of dubious quality, especially for some nations and wars[1] during the nineteenth century and early twentieth centuries. Sometimes, a published figure turned out to be based on someone's educated guess rather than on any systematic information-gathering procedures, as in the case of some population figures for China.[2] On other occasions, the wording in the sources may be vague or misleading, as with Latin American population statistics which sometimes appear to omit the Indian population,[3] or in the case of some questionable military budget figures which may refer to appropriations rather than amounts actually dispensed. Finally, in some cases there is reason to suspect deliberate falsification; there are of course many reasons why governments may wish to conceal information about industrial or military capability, and in the age of mass electorates even population figures are ofttimes subject to political distortions. Of course, wherever possible an attempt was made to compensate for such biases, but a) since these errors are often difficult to discover, some may have gone undetected, and b) even when discovered it is difficult to determine what compensation should be made, the task being hindered by the very lack of information which forced reliance on an unsatisfactory estimate in the first place. In short, it is most unlikely that *all* of the raw data are free from such errors, even to a first approximation.

A second possible source of error concerns the spacing of the observations. Since data on the indices are generated at five year intervals, there is always the possibility that a different choice of collection dates would have yielded different values, or that the values obtained are not representative of those which would have been generated by more frequent sampling. As noted in Chapter 3, this does not pose a serious danger to the reliability of tl.e results so long as the values of the indices change rather slowly, and indeed it was discovered that this condition was usually met. But obviously, exceptions did occur; wars, political upheavals, economic cycles, and epidemics occasionally resulted in fairly large changes in our index values over a period much shorter than five years. Although some attempt was made to minimize this difficulty by eliminating the large and rapid fluctuations in the independent variables associated with the largest wars, it still cannot be said with complete certainty that these quinquennial measurements have not omitted or distorted important trends in the data.

Error Sensitivities

Even if the precautions noted above and in Chapter 3 *have* been successful in reducing errors in the data to a relatively low level, there are three reasons why such errors might still have produced major distortions in the observed results.

First, despite the length of the time-period examined here, the effective N is rather small, never rising above twenty-seven and occasionally falling as low as sixteen. To be sure, as reported in the previous chapter, it is unlikely that the findings could have been produced solely by chance variation or "random" error. However, significance tests can say nothing about the likely effect of *systematic* error. Obviously the smaller the N, the more sensitive the findings will be to any such contamination, since fluctuations in fewer data points are required to produce an important alteration in the observed coefficients. With N's as small as those employed here, the dangers posed by systematic error are very great indeed; if there were, for example, a major error in one of the indices for even a single half-decade period, serious perturbations might be produced in the reported findings.

A second reason why these findings may be quite sensitive to error concerns the nature of the independent variables themselves; in both cases they are *derived* variables, not measured directly from raw data values, but calculated as the first differences between raw indices suitably transformed. As a consequence, even if the raw data are accurate within tolerable limits, the final measures may not be; first differences will be small by comparison with the original data values yet subject to the same absolute magnitude of error.

A third factor rendering the results of the multivariate analysis still more vulnerable to error contamination is the high degree of intercorrelation between and among the various indicators of the independent variables. While it is inevitable that some such correlation will exist, here it is often quite strong, and this poses problems for both stepwise regression and path analysis.

In regression equations, it may generate a pathological degree of multicollinearity. As noted in Chapter 4, when two independent variables are highly intercorrelated, it becomes difficult to distinguish between them empirically. Therefore, any calculations which attempt to determine their relative impact on the dependent variable will be sensitive to very small movements in the data points, and thus vulnerable to error (Blalock, 1962, pp. 87-90; Forbes and Tufte, 1968). In the case of *stepwise* regression, this means that the choice of which indices of the variables to include, and which to exclude from the equations may end up being largely a function of error variance.

Although it appears in a somewhat different form, using dependence analysis does not permit us to escape this problem. While we have not spoken of confidence limits with regard to this technique,[4] it is true in general that the higher the correlations between the independent variables in our equations, (technically, the more "ill-conditioned" the matrix) the more the dependence coefficients will vary with small fluctuations in the correlations. This means, of course, that in such cases the observed magnitudes of the dependence coefficients will be highly sensitive to data error.

An Assessment

Despite the serious consequences which data error may have for the findings, it is worth stressing that this by no means implies that the conclusions which might be drawn from them are *ipso facto* dubious. First, not all of the data are uniformly problematic; such indices as urban population may indeed often represent only good guesses, but, at the other end of the scale, the index of nation-months of war begun is almost certainly quite accurate (Singer and Small, 1972). Second, let us recall that it is only a plausible inference—and not a proven fact—that data error may have influenced the results. The only point being made is that despite the magnitude of the observed relationships, we cannot claim to have demonstrated *conclusively* the existence of a statistical association between and among our various indices. Unless these findings are found to hold when different data are used—based on different temporal domains, intervals, and sources of information—we can only attach a limited degree of confidence to them.

Validity

That these findings demonstrate the existence of connections between status inconsistency, status mobility, and war may be questioned on grounds of validity as well as those of reliability. That is, even if the data should prove to be virtually error-free, it is always open to question whether or not the indices employed "truly" measure the concepts they purport to, and, consequently, whether the statistical relationships among them represent genuine evidence for our hypotheses. Given the nature of the indices employed in this study, we cannot dismiss the validity problem lightly.

International War

The indices of our dependent variable—the number of nation-months of war begun and the number of battle fatalities from war involvement begun in each five-year period in the international system—appear to hold out the fewest validity problems. Even they, however, have one important weakness (Singer and Small, 1972): the slight difference between the coding rules used for inter-state (intrasystemic) wars, and those used for colonial and imperial (extra-systemic) wars. In the case of the former, the nation-month and the battle-death indices are computed as the sum of all the participants' scores; in the case of the latter, only the totals for the participating state-members were summed. Since the purpose of the indices was to measure the amount of war experienced by state-members of the international system, this decision to exclude the battle-deaths and nation-months of nonmember belligerents may be quite reasonable, but it clearly results in an undervaluing of the severity and magnitude of extrasystemic war.

National Capability

Rather more serious questions of validity are posed with regard to the indices of national capability status used to construct the independent variables. Indeed, a case could be made that they reflect a nation's true power base only in a very limited and incomplete fashion.

To begin with, even within each of the three categories of capability measured in this study—demographic, military, and economic—the indices may not be very faithful measures. First, as noted in Chapter 3, the number of people in a nation—or even in its cities—means less than the number of productive age and the distribution of skills amongst them. Second, iron and steel production may reflect the volume of industrial production, but obviously does not touch on other important aspects of a nation's economic power base such as economic self-sufficiency, efficiency of production technology, and the distribution of economic production amongst the industrial, agricultural, military, and consumer sectors. Third, military capacity is not only a function of the number of effectives and the monetary resources that have been allocated to them, but is also dependent upon the way these raw "givens" are translated into specific capabilities via training, organization, and weapons acquisitions.

But even granting the adequacy of our indices as measures of their respective power bases, it is by no means certain that these three categories are, by themselves, sufficient to measure overall national capability. Many would argue, for example, that efficiency of social organization and political unity (Organski, 1968, pp. 170-83; Morgenthau, 1967, pp. 132-4; Rosecrance, 1963, pp. 225-6) are equally important components of national power base, since they determine what percentage of a nation's total resource base is in fact available for use and disposition by the political elite.

Attributed Status

A similar although much less severe critique may be made of our index of attributed status, national diplomatic importance; once again, it is not that the index is misleading as far as it goes, but that it perhaps does not go far enough. Although the number of diplomatic missions sent to a nation probably reflects many different aspects of its standing vis-à-vis the other members of the system, under some circumstances a nation's attributed status may be better reflected in other ways, such as the willingness of others to enter into military alliances with it (Singer and Small, 1965), to join common intergovernmental organizations (Wallace and Singer, 1970), to sign trade or economic treaties with it, or otherwise behave in a positive or cooperative fashion towards that nation.

Validity: Summary

Since the foregoing subsections have painted a very sombre picture, it may be wise to end on a somewhat more balanced note. While the questions of index validity raised above represent *potential* difficulties, they are by no means *proven* ones; it is more than likely, for example, that social organization and industrial production, or manpower skills and urban population, are so highly correlated that more sophisticated indices are not needed. The point is only that we do not yet *know* this to be so, and hence, it cannot be asserted that the hypotheses of this study have been definitively confirmed. Only on the basis of further tests using alternative indices could such a claim be made with complete confidence.

Spuriousness and Causal Inference

If we cannot be completely certain that the observed findings represent true associations between our variables, we can be even less certain that they indicate the presence of *causal* relationships. Statistical associations between variables may be wholly spurious, mere artifacts of genuine causal relationships linking each of the variables in question with some additional variable not included in the analysis. Only to the extent that we can discount or control for such exogenous factors can we infer causality from association.

It was in recognition of this difficulty that status mobility was introduced into the analysis. We demonstrated that most of the observed relationships between status inconsistency and war were not artifacts of status mobility, allowing us to have more confidence in the results than would have been justified in the case of mere bivariate correlations.

However, there may be other important exogenous factors we have not controlled for, and which—given the scarcity of hard evidence about the relationships within the international system—may offer alternative explanations of our findings. There is little point in exploring these in great detail, since they would lead us very far afield, and, in the context of the present inquiry, would be almost wholly speculative. Nonetheless, to illustrate the need for caution in interpreting the findings, and to suggest some possible directions for further research, it is worth outlining briefly four possible alternative models which are compatible with the relationships found in this study, but which do not presuppose causal connections between our independent and dependent variables.

System Size

First of all, the observed associations between status mobility, status inconsistency, and war might to some extent be accounted for by variations in system size. On the one hand, it might be reasoned that the amount of international war begun in any given five-year period depends on the number of nations in the system. That is, *ceteris paribus*, the more nations that were members of the international system, the more nation-months of war would be fought, and the larger the number of battle fatalities that would be suffered. On the other hand, it would be reasonable to expect (once again, other things being equal) that the larger and more diverse the international system, the greater the likelihood that the rates of change in capability and attributed status would differ between and among nations, and the greater the probability of inconsistencies between these two status continua. Since the subset of the international system included in this study expands from thirteen in 1825 to sixty-one in 1960, and since status inconsistency and status mobility values do indeed seem to show a generally upward secular trend, the danger that the observed relationships between the variables are largely functions of an expanding international system would seem, on the face of it, a fairly serious one.

But while the possibility that changes in system size account for at least a portion of the variance cannot be ruled out entirely, two facts would appear to attenuate the risk considerably. First, it has been discovered empirically[5] that there is in fact very little relationship between the size of the international system in any given period and the amount of war begun in that period; no statistically significant associations are observed in any of the subperiods under study, and the correlation is very low for the 140-year period as a whole. Second, as was detailed in Chapter 3, the indices of status inconsistency and status mobility were normalized precisely so as to take account of increasing system size.

Technology

Another possible line of reasoning which might lead to the conclusion that these relationships are spurious begins with the many important changes in technology which have occurred over the 140 years examined here. On the one hand, most writers have asserted that such technological changes have exercised an important influence on at least the *severity*—if not the magnitude—of international war during this period (Wright, 1965, p. 242), citing as examples the devastating toll taken by such innovations as the machine gun in World War I and the airplane in World War II. On the other hand, technological change may no doubt be partly responsible as well for high differential rates of capability change during the latter part of the period studied, since technical innovation clearly did not diffuse equally throughout the international system. Thus, it is possible that our relationships are, in part, artifacts of the growth and diffusion of technology over time.

However, there is again some evidence to suggest that this is not very likely. While the status mobility scores do indeed show an overall increase over the 145 years under study, this is not the case for international war; neither war index has any significant relationship with time (Singer and Small, 1972, Chapter 15). This does not rule out entirely the possibility that the observed relationships are artifacts of technological change, since innovation by no means occurred in a smooth or linear fashion, but would seem to render it a much less important consideration.

Polarization

Turning specifically to the relationship between status inconsistency and war, it might also be possible to account for the findings in terms of the polarization of the international system. We saw in Chapter 2 how, under normal circumstances, the status expectations held by a nation both for itself and others were generally set in terms of national capabilities. As a consequence, attributed status, other things being equal, will be roughly proportional to these capabilities.

But if most nations are grouped into two or more mutually exclusive, tightly bound groups defined in ideological, military, or economic terms, a nation's reputational status may depend far less on its capabilities than on the nature and strength of its group affiliation. For one thing, a nation belonging to a large and important bloc would, *ceteris paribus*, have a higher attributed status score than one from a smaller bloc regardless of its own capabilities, as can be readily seen if we compare scores for, say, Belgium and Poland in 1955. Second, nations which are quasi-autonomous or neutral as between blocs may have, other things being considered, a higher attributed status than those which are tightly bound, as would seem to have been the case with France under de Gaulle. Third, regardless of its bloc affiliation, a nation with a high strategic value for whatever reason is likely to enjoy a relatively higher status during periods of high polarization. Thus, when the international system is highly polarized, there are likely to be more inconsistencies between capability and attributed status than when the structure of the system is less coagulated.

Furthermore, numerous writers have argued that there exists an important connection between the level of polarization in the system and the genesis of war (Singer and Deutsch, 1968; Singer and Small, 1968; Kaplan, 1957, pp. 43-5). While some would argue that polarization reduces the *frequency* of war (Waltz, 1969, p. 312), most would agree that it increases the magnitude and severity of conflicts which do occur, by drawing additional nations into limited struggles and reducing the "damping effect" of the neutrals and the uninvolved. Therefore, since a high level of polarization may lead by separate processes both to status inconsistency and to international war, it may well be that the observed relationship between these two variables is in large part an artifact of fluctuations in the degree of polarization among the nations in the international system.

Economic Development

Returning to the relationship between differential status mobility and war, a fourth alternative explanatory model might be constructed with reference to the rate of economic development taking place within nations. Because such development—like the technological change that precedes it—progresses at widely varying rates among the members of the system, and since it is associated with changes on both the industrial and demographic dimensions of capability, (Kuznets, 1966, Chapter 2) it is almost certain to result in differential status mobility.

However, it may not be this differential mobility *per se* which leads to war, but rather the changes that a rapid rate of economic development create *within* some nations. It is possible to conceive of at least three such changes which may markedly increase the likelihood that a nation will become involved in war. For one thing, there is evidence that development often leads to political instability (Tanter and Midlarsky, 1967) which may in turn lead a ruling elite into foreign adventure to distract potential opposition, or, conversely, may invite foreign invasion and intervention (Wilkenfeld, 1968). Second, development might result in the generation of surplus industrial capability which may tempt a policy elite to build a larger military establishment, the existence of which might in turn enhance the probability of war. Finally, development may lead to—or be accompanied by—the rise of aggressive, chiliastic political leadership whose actions may be such as to enhance the probability of war involvement. Thus, the observed relationship between status mobility and war may be only an artifact of increases in national war involvement induced by a high rate of economic development in particular states.

Although these lines of reasoning represent no more than plausible hypotheses, the point is that we are in no position to make more than very tentative causal inferences on the basis of the present findings. To make such statements with confidence, a number of other variables would have to be introduced into the analysis.

Insufficient Explanation

Even if we were willing to interpret the findings as evidence of both association and causation, it is worth emphasizing that we cannot infer from the magnitude of the correlations, dependence coefficients, and multiple R^2's that status inconsistency and status mobility represent the only—or even the most important—factors predicting to the onset of war. While one can do little more than hypothesize and speculate about possible error contamination in the data, or possible exogenous influences which would make the findings spurious, there is clear *evidence* that factors other than status inconsistency and mobility have an important influence on the severity and magnitude of war.

First, with very few exceptions, the proportion of the variance *not* explained by our two independent variables is far too high to be accounted for by mere error; even in the most favorable cases, this percentage is between one-quarter and one-third of the total, and in the typical case it would appear to be about one-half. Moreover, note that the combined effect of the various indices is not even statistically significant in some cases. For some time-periods and lags, multivariate equations can only be constructed for one of the two indices of war begun, and in no case was the amount of variance explained by each variable taken separately more than 52%, with more typical values ranging between 20% and 25%.

A second indication that other important explanatory variables remain to be discovered was the presence of some degree of autocorrelation in the residuals. First, as we saw, the Durbin-Watson statistics showed some conclusive evidence of serially correlated residuals along with several inconclusive[6] findings. Second, the magnitude of the observed relationships does not increase or decrease in a straightforward fashion with changing time lags, as would be expected if the error terms were not correlated with one another; this suggests the presence of at least *some* autocorrelation. As Johnston (1963, pp. 177-8) has pointed out, this is almost always due to an important explanatory variable being omitted from the equations; since the values of such a variable will usually not be serially independent, its inclusion in the error term will generate autocorrelated residuals.

Moreover, the existence of such serial correlation provides still another argument against the claim that status inconsistency and mobility represent the strongest influences on war. As noted in Chapter 4, autocorrelation—particularly when combined with time lags—is almost certain to result in an *overestimate* of the multiple R^2. Thus, there is a distinct possibility that our two variables explain even less of the variance than the one-third to two-thirds appearing in the equations; this, of course, reinforces the argument for the inclusion of additional variables.

In short, even if it is proved conclusively that status inconsistency and status mobility do have an important causal influence on the amount of international war begun, the two variables can in no sense be said to represent a *sufficient* explanation for the genesis of war. Therefore, propositions seeking to explain war on the basis of these variables alone must necessarily be incomplete and partial.

Additional Indices

We have seen that the inferences that can be made from these findings may be limited in several ways by the absence of predictor variables other than status inconsistency and status mobility. They are limited as well by the omission of other types of status inconsistency and status mobility based on other national attributes. Although it was argued in Chapter 2 that national capability and the standing attributed to a nation by other system-members are probably central dimensions in a nation's status set, they are clearly not the only important ones, and may not even be the most important. Other national status rankings of direct and ongoing interest to both decision-making elites and their supporting clientele include those based on such factors as: economic advantages enjoyed in dealings with other nations, material standard of living, economic development, available capital resources, territorial possessions, and cultural, religious, and racial identity (Galtung, 1964, pp. 117-9). Thus, there are probably many other important types of status inconsistency and mobility beside those measured by the indices employed here, and it is quite possible that the inclusion of these different types would lead us to modify the assessment of our hypotheses constructed on the basis of the present findings.

First, it might be found that other forms of status inconsistency and mobility have little or no statistical association with war. Some intimation that this might be the case can be gleaned from the previous chapter; there, we noted that mobility on *attributed* status did not appear to be associated with war, and status inconsistencies between industrial capability and attributed status seemed to yield no better a result. If this pattern were to be reinforced by examination of other indices of inconsistency and mobility, we could hardly assert the existence of a *general* association between these two variables and the severity and magnitude of war. Rather, our claims would have to be limited to specific status dimensions.

Second, we might, on the contrary, discover that these other indices were *better* predictors than the ones employed here, and that, by themselves or in combination with the indices used here, they explain an even higher proportion of the variance than could be accounted for above. If so, we could not only be more confident in inferring the existence of general relationships between our independent and dependent variables, but there would be less need to qualify our assessment of the validity and reliability of our indices.

Third, it may be that different indices would show a different *type* of relationship. For one thing, the use of different measures might yield relationships which were optimized by employing a shorter time lag, suggesting, for example, that inconsistency between capability and living standards has a much more direct impact on the onset of war than the inconsistencies measured here. Or, it might be that other forms of inconsistency affect war during different historical epochs; as noted in Chapter 2, we might expect that inconsistencies between capability and territorial acquisition would be important only during the earlier part of our 140-year period.

In short, inferences from these findings must take account of the possibility that many different relationships exist between status inconsistency, differential status mobility, and the severity and magnitude of war, and that we are not entirely justified in speaking in general terms about these relationships until our results have been compared with those of future studies.

The National Level of Analysis

There is another sense in which this study fails to examine fully the relationships between the independent and dependent variables. All of the variables have been measured, and all of the statistical tests run, at the level of the international system as a whole; for reasons amply detailed above, the relationships between the variables at the national level of analysis have not been examined. This places two limitations on the interpretations which may be put forward concerning the observed relationships.

First and foremost, it means—as we noted—that we cannot directly infer the existence of a relationship between any particular nation's status mobility or inconsistency score and its war involvement from these results. Such an interpretation of the findings is ruled out by the problem of so-called ecological fallacy (Robinson, 1950). Since our indices are aggregated over the system as a whole, it is possible that the countries which exhibit a high degree of inconsistency and mobility are different from those which have been involved in war. As will be apparent in the next chapter, there are sometimes *indirect* ways of making such inferences, but they are inevitably weaker and less reliable than had our hypotheses been tested at the national level.

Second, as a corollary to this point, testing the hypotheses at the system level makes it impossible to determine in which *direction* inconsistency and mobility have their greatest influence. If there is inconsistency between capability and attributed status rankings over the system as a whole, this implies the existence of *two* types of inconsistent nations: those whose capability ranking is higher than their attributed status; and those whose attributed importance ranks higher than their capability. As Hernes (1969) and Galtung (1969) have noted, it is by no means certain that *both* types of nations will be equally prone to war involvement. Correspondingly, the existence of a high degree of differential status mobility in the system implies that there exist both upward and downwardly mobile nations. Once again, it is very unlikely that both types of mobility are equally conducive to war involvement, at least not via the same processes. In examining our hypotheses solely at the system level, we cannot distinguish between the effects of these distinct types of inconsistency and mobility.

Alternative Causal Directions

Our findings do not represent an adequate examination of the relationships between and among our variables in one final sense: we have not examined the possibility that the relationships run in different directions. As Forbes and Tufte (1968) have emphasized, techniques such as multiple regression and dependence analysis do not by themselves determine the *direction* of causal relationships, but only allow us to solve for their magnitude once this direction has been assumed. Here we have assumed that status mobility may affect status inconsistency, and that status mobility and status inconsistency may both affect war. However, there are several possible alternative causal directions.

To begin with, the relationship between status inconsistency and war may operate in reverse as well. Although one line of reasoning put forth above argued that war may be the product of a desire to *reduce* status inconsistency, the termination of major hostilities may see inconsistency greatly increased. On the one hand, the inevitable process of rewarding the winners and punishing the losers is likely to result in *upward* shifts in attributed status for the former, with a *downward* shift being the probable lot of the latter. Thus, if the losers experienced inconsistency to begin with, the war would only result in its exacerbation. On the other hand, the profound disturbances created by major wars are almost certain to alter the relative *capabilities* of the nations in the system, quite possibly leading to the same result.

Second, war may create rapid mobility as well, either as a product of the conflict itself, or as the result of the postwar period of recovery in which those nations most strongly affected by the war will experience the greatest relative change in capability.

Third, while it has been assumed that status mobility may affect the amount of status inconsistency, the reverse process is also quite plausible. If we assume that nations which are inconsistent are not content to remain in that state but will attempt to move upward on their low dimension, status mobility is as probable an outcome of inconsistency as war.

Finally, we have assumed mobility on the various capability and attributed status dimensions to be independent factors affecting status inconsistency. But if, as the arguments set forth in Chapter 2 would suggest, there is an inherent tendency towards "status equilibration" in the international system, it is more than likely that rates of mobility on the different status continua are reciprocally related. Thus, even if we are justified in making causal inferences about our results, we cannot assume these to be the *only* possible links between the variables; further tests may reveal that relationships in other directions are of equal or even greater significance.

Having dealt with some of the conclusions that *cannot* be drawn from this study, we may now turn to those that can; what new knowledge do our findings yield, and in what respects does it complement or contradict other hypotheses, beliefs, and evidence about the nature of the international system in general and war in particular?

Notes

1. A detailed discussion of the accuracy problem as it pertains to the *dependent* variable is to be found in Singer and Small (1972, Chapter 3).

2. A footnote in Almanach de Gotha (1886, p. 645) provides an interesting commentary on the method of arriving at some of these figures: "Dans le 'Journal of the Statis. Society' de mars 1884, Londres, Sir R. Temple fait l'essai de parvenir, d'une manière indirecte, à la notion juste de la population de la Chine. Il compare chaque province chinoise avec une province de l'Inde anglaise de la même nature, et il trouve de cette manière le chiffre 282, 161, 923."

3. For example, after recording its population estimates for Peru for the year 1896, the STATESMAN'S YEARBOOK (1909, p. 1098) remarks: "There are, besides, many uncivilized indians, but their numbers are absolutely unknown."

4. As Turner and Stevens (1959) point out, the problem of determining the statistical significance of dependence coefficients is extremely complex, and often exact confidence limits cannot be obtained for multiple-stage paths.

5. As reported to the author by John Stuckey of the Correlates of War Project.

6. Since the Durbin-Watson statistic does not produce exact confidence limits for serially correlated errors, the test result can often be neither the acceptance nor the rejection of the null hypothesis, especially with a small N. Only conclusive findings were reported here.

6 Interpreting the Findings

Introduction

In the previous chapter, detailed attention was given to the many ways in which the findings could signify something other than support for the basic hypotheses of this study. Such caution was not misplaced; as the reader is by now well aware, the lines of reasoning which led to the selection of hypotheses, concepts, indices, methods of data generation, and techniques of analysis all passed through intellectual *terra incognita* at many points. This made it imperative to point out that findings whose direction, magnitude, and consistency would be conclusive in a field where data-based evidence and systematic research methods were better developed can only be considered tentative in the present context.

But precisely because the study of international politics is so "data-poor" it will not do to substitute Type II error for Type I, and shrink from a full interpretation of our findings. On the contrary, the very paucity of data-based evidence about the international system—and particularly about the causes of international war—makes it imperative that every shred of meaning be gleaned from what is discovered. This is especially important in the present case, because, as we shall see, these findings have important implications which go beyond the confirmation of our specific hypotheses, and touch on many different facets of our knowledge and belief in the discipline. In dealing with the interpretation of the specific results, therefore, a much broader question will be constantly in the foreground, namely, to what extent do these findings support—or, alternatively, disconfirm—*other* beliefs, hypotheses, theoretical propositions, and explanatory models about the international system, especially as these pertain to the origins of international war?

Of course, in assessing the findings it will often be discovered that the evidence does not point in a single direction; in most cases, several plausible interpretations or competing models might be offered. Where this is the case the alternatives will be presented, along with a) the evidence for and against each, and b) a summary of what additional evidence would be required to confirm each interpretation. In this way, the reader will be able to make her or his own assessment of the evidence independently of the author, and further research will be guided by pointing to the deficiencies in our knowledge.

The findings shall be examined under four main headings. First, we shall examine, and attempt to account for, the differences between the two major patterns observed in the findings. Does the apparent existence of both a *direct* link between status mobility and war, and an *indirect* link via status inconsistency, imply that two distinct factors contributing to the onset of war have been identified, or are these apparently distinct patterns merely the product of some statistical artifact? Second, what are some of the more plausible causal sequences which would account for the existence of a *direct* link between status mobility and war, and what are the arguments for and against each? Third, to what extent do the findings support our earlier hunches about the intervening variables linking status inconsistency and war? What are the strengths and disadvantages of alternative models linking these two variables? In a final chapter, we shall attempt to discover what implications, if any, these results have for the efforts of statesmen and others to *reduce* the amount of war in the international system?

Two Basic Models—Alternative or Complementary?

Clearly, the most striking finding reported in Chapter 4 was the apparent existence of two different types of causal connection among status mobility, status inconsistency, and war. On the one hand, when indices of *demographic* or *military* capability were used, the causal sequence appeared to run as follows: status mobility acted to produce status inconsistency, which in turn acted to increase the magnitude and severity of war. On the other hand, when *industrial* capability was used, a quite different pattern was discovered; differential change in capability predicted *directly* to the amount of war, and, combined with differential change in attributed status, predicted to status inconsistency as well. In this case, however, there was little or no connection between status inconsistency and war. There are two distinct strategies which may be pursued in accounting for this difference: we may either proceed from the assumption that these two findings do not represent a genuine difference, but are merely some artifact of our measurement or analysis procedures, or we may assume that they do in fact identify two separate causal sequences. What evidence do we possess which would permit us to decide between these alternative interpretations?

Difference as Artifact (I): Industrial Capacity as Sole Influence

One line of reasoning which might lead to the conclusion that the supposed difference between the two observed patterns is a mere artifact would run as follows. According to one school of thought, the most crucial dimension of national capability is sheer economic capacity (Organski, 1961, pp. 208-15; Fucks, 1965). Those who adhere to this point of view argue that it is changes in national positions on this economic dimension that control changes on all other rankings, and are thus ultimately responsible for governing relations between nations. If we accept this, it could be argued that the relationships discovered when industrial capacity was used as the index of national capability represent the true pattern of causal connections, and consequently that the relationship between status inconsistency and war is spurious throughout.

To support this argument, one might point to two significant features in the results. First, there is the extremely strong relationship observed between mobility on the industrial dimension and amount of war begun ten to fifteen years later. The magnitude of this relationship exceeds that which links status inconsistency and war, no matter which index of the former variable is used. Thus, if we control for differential mobility on the industrial capability dimension, the relationships between status inconsistency on the demographic and military dimensions vanish as well.

Second, if industrial capacity were indeed the only capability dimension to have an important influence on war, we would expect mobility on urban population and military expenditures to show a greater degree of association with war than mobility on total population and military personnel, since these last two indices are less closely related to industrial capacity. As we see from Table 4-2, such is indeed the case.

But, while this line of reasoning has some surface plausibility, and apparently can account for some aspects of the findings, several telling counter arguments may be made.

First and foremost, the assertion that industrial capacity is the only important power base dimension is only a plausible hypothesis—not a proven fact—and is hotly contested to boot. Some (Claude, 1962, p. 6) have argued strongly to the contrary, asserting that other dimensions of capability—particularly the military one—exercise an autonomous influence on relationships and behavior in the international system. If this indeed is the case, it would not be a legitimate procedure to hold status mobility measured in terms of industrial capability constant when examining the relationship between war and status inconsistency measured in demographic or military terms (Blalock, 1962, pp. 67, 83-7; Greenstein, 1967).

Second, the argument is not only theoretically questionable, but does not square with another important feature of the results. If the very strong relationships obtained using status inconsistency measured in demographic and military terms are indeed spurious artifacts of mobility on industrial capability, and do not represent a true causal link, the inconsistencies must be the *result* of such mobility. For this to be true, it would be necessary to posit a causal link passing through status mobility on either of the other capability dimensions and/or the attributed status dimension. For example, if inconsistencies between demographic capability and attributed status are caused by differential mobility on industrial capability, this can only be because mobility on *this* dimension leads to mobility on either demographic or attributed status, which in turn produces the inconsistency. If either of these two-step causal chains existed, we would expect that the correlations between industrial mobility and mobility on the demographic, military, or attributed status dimensions to be *greater* than the correlations between industrial mobility and status inconsistency (Blalock, 1962, p. 73). In fact we find them to be *less* in virtually every case, suggesting that the status inconsistency-war relationship is not an artifact but an independent influence on war.

In sum, then, it is hard to see how *all* our results can be accounted for by differential industrial mobility, no matter how strong its relationship with war may be. This is not to say, of course, that it has no influence; as we shall see later, several arguments can be adduced to support the hypothesis that it does indeed have a strong independent effect. However, it seems fairly clear that the discrepancy in our results cannot be explained by the action of this variable alone.

Difference as Artifact (II): Other
Status Inconsistencies

There is a second way, however, in which the difference in results obtained using different indices might be due to an artifact of measurement. It may be that differential industrial mobility (just as with differential demographic and differential military mobility) does indeed act *indirectly* on war by increasing status inconsistency, but that in the case of the industrial dimension it is a different sort of inconsistency that acts as an intervening variable. We speculated in Chapter 3 that inconsistencies between capability and rank-dimensions *other* than reputational status may be of much greater importance, and this may well be the case with regard to industrial capability. It is more than plausible, for example, that inconsistencies between industrial capability and relative economic advantage would exercise a considerably greater disturbing influence on national behavior than inconsistency between industrial capability and reputational status.

Obviously, unlike the previous explanation, we have no definite evidence one way or the other about the accuracy of this line of reasoning. Only by actually constructing indices which measure such inconsistencies could we directly validate or disconfirm this explanation. However, there is one piece of indirect evidence which makes it at least rather doubtful that such an intervening factor exists.

If status inconsistency of whatever sort *is* an intervening variable between differential industrial mobility and war, it must be the case that the correlation coefficients between such status inconsistency and the amount of international war begun are noticeably *larger* than those between industrial mobility and war begun for the same time lag (Blalock, 1962, p. 73). Since these latter coefficients already range from a low of .58 to a high of .72, the bivariate relationship between war and our hypothetical intervening variable must, in some cases, approach unity. While it may be attractive to speculate on the existence of a relationship of this magnitude, it can scarcely be considered a very likely possibility.

Reconciling the Differences—An
Alternative Approach

Thus far we have examined two possible ways of reconciling the different patterns observed in the results by attempting to reduce them to a single causal sequence. This was found to be a difficult task; in the one case, verification or supporting evidence from further research would be required, and in the other it proved difficult or impossible to fit the model to the findings.

There is, however, a different way of proceeding; we may assume that the two patterns identified represent two genuinely distinct causal sequences. As noted in Chapter 4, one important piece of evidence would appear to support such an assumption. When entered into a regression equation together, industrial mobility and status inconsistency measured in demographic and military terms consistently explained a greater proportion of the variance in the amount of war begun than any other combination of indicators. If we assume these indices are the crucial ones, the obvious question is: why does the status inconsistency index based on industrial production have so little apparent influence?

Perhaps the most plausible answer might be framed in terms of the traditional beliefs of statesmen concerning the national attributes which go to make up national capability. There is a good deal of anecdotal evidence to suggest that national decision-makers have tended to stress the demographic and military dimensions of a nation's power base in evaluating national capability, giving relatively less emphasis to industrial production. On the one hand, the persistent overevaluation of the importance of Russia's large population throughout the nineteenth century (Tuchman, 1962, Chapter 5), the concern expressed in France during the interwar period at the low birthrate, the infamous Nazi program of encouraging Aryan fecundity, and—in the contemporary setting—the reluctance of many Third World leaders to introduce birth control programs, all attest to the strength and persistence of the belief that population equals power. On the other hand, we see an historical tendency, visible in both the nineteenth and twentieth centuries, to underrate the importance of economic capacity in evaluating such nations as Britain and the U.S., which are highly industrialized but lack large standing armies. If these beliefs about national capability have indeed been as well entrenched as these examples would suggest, we might expect that discrepancies between demographic or military capability and attributed status would be far more important influences on national behavior than discrepancies between attributed status and industrial capability.

It must be admitted, however, that this line of reasoning is not wholly convincing for two reasons. First, it is easy to point to counter examples which seem to illustrate a deep appreciation of the importance of industrial capacity; the most obvious are the programs of rapid industrialization undertaken by such major powers as Germany, Japan, the Soviet Union, and, most recently, China. Second, this interpretation does not square with one other feature of the results. During the earliest portion of the temporal domain, the indices of status inconsistency which best predict to war are those which reflect the gross size of nations, total population and the sheer number of military effectives. Moving to a later period, however, we find that indices reflecting the more modern and sophisticated aspects of capability, (urban population and military expenditures) become equally powerful predictors. This would seem to suggest, contrary to the argument advanced above, that national decision-makers *have* taken cognizance of the changing nature of national capability. It would seem, then, that a definitive explanation for this apparent failure of the status inconsistency hypothesis in the case of industrial capability will have to await further study.

But if it is difficult to account for the lack of a status inconsistency—war link when the iron and steel production index was used, there is no lack of alternative models to explain the existence of a *direct* link between mobility on this index and war, and it is to these that we now turn.

Status Mobility and War—Three
Alternative Models

The Balance of Power Model

One possible explanation for the observed connection between differential changes in industrial capability and war might be framed in terms of the classical balance of power model. According to this model, peace and stability in the international system depend upon the checks to national ambition and aggressiveness induced by a delicate balance among the relative capabilities of competing, fluctuating coalitions of nations (Claude, 1962, pp. 42-43). If this is an accurate portrayal of the state of affairs prevailing in the system, rapid changes in the relative power of nations induced by differential rates of industrial growth may lead to a breakdown of the balance, resulting in the unleashing of national aggressiveness and war. But while the balance of power model might thus appear to account for a connection between differential industrial growth and war, there are three important considerations which argue against its acceptance.

First, the balance of power model as it is usually conceived does not refer so much to a balance of capability defined in economic terms as it does to an equilibrium among armed forces (Morgenthau, 1967, p. 174). Although increased economic capacity may presage or permit increases in armed might, this represents only a hypothetical threat to the balance of power; what counts is that the actual configuration of relative military capacity, in being or readily mobilizable, be such as to deter aggression on all sides. Thus, if the balance of power hypothesis represented the true explanation for the present findings, we might expect to find some evidence of a direct link between industrial mobility and war, but we would expect a much stronger direct relationship between war and mobility on the military capability dimension. Such is not the case, as we saw from Table 4-4.

Second, most writers who adhere to the balance of power approach would agree that the greatest danger to peace and stability posed by rapid shifts in relative national capabilities occurs in the short run. In the long run, it is argued, nations may compensate for such changes by rearranging their patterns of alignment. For example, if one power begins to augment its strength at too great a rate, several of its neighbors may form a defensive alliance against it. But before such equilibrating and compensatory mechanisms come into play, an "unbalanced" nation may seize the opportunity to commit aggression (Gulick, 1955, pp. 67-70). Thus, the model predicts that the strongest link between differential capability change and war should be found with a *short* time-lag, and, once again, precisely the opposite was discovered. In order for the balance of power model to account for the existence of a relationship with a ten to fifteen year time-lag, it would be necessary to assume that the nations of the system were not aware of important changes in their relative capabilities for as much as a decade or more. While this might be plausible in the case of those powers situated some distance from the European heartland—for example, the United States, Japan, and to a lesser extent, Russia—events such as the Anglo-German naval arms race demonstrate how acutely sensitive nations can be to increments in relative capability. Moreover, the existence of such a high degree of sensitivity is usually a basic premise of the advocates of the balance of power approach (Morgenthau, pp. 187-90).

Finally, even if we were to disregard these objections, there remains yet another difficulty in applying the balance of power model to the findings. If the model were indeed the correct one, the predicted direction of the relationship between differential capability change and war would not *always* be positive, but sometimes null or even negative. For, while differential changes in capability may *upset* a given balance by giving an inordinately large capability to one nation or coalition, it may under different circumstances *strengthen* the balance by shoring up a weaker coalition, or even lead to a new balance by permitting the creation of a new and more stable pattern of alliances. If, therefore, the balance of power model is in principle compatible with *any* relationship between differential capability and war measured over the system as a whole, it can scarcely be claimed that the present study adduces any evidence one way or the other concerning its plausibility. In short, the balance of power model *may* account for the observed relationship between differential industrial growth rates and war, but in order to demonstrate it, further tests—using indices which measure the degree of "balance" in the system—would be necessary.

The Power Transition Model

A second explanatory model which may account for this observed relationship is the "power transition" model articulated by Organski (1968, Chapter 14). In contradiction to the balance of power model, which attributed the onset of war to unbalanced capabilities between and among nations or groups of nations, this view holds that stability can only be obtained when one nation or coalition in the system has a *preponderance* of capability. When the relationships of subordination and superordination between and among the nations of the system on a scale of capabilities are clearly established, warfare is less likely because each nation "knows its place." But when a nation or group of nations moves upward on the capability dimension and begins to approach the strength of the dominant nation or coalition, there is likely to be a struggle for dominance resulting in major war. Thus, the power transition model would predict that differential rates of capability change would lead to an increased probability of conflict, and, in several ways, this hypothesis fits the observed results better than the balance of power model.

First, it seems to account more precisely for the particular *index* of differential capability change having a direct influence on war. Although at one point Organski comes close to claiming that the demographic component of capability is the most crucial (1968, pp. 144-6), he ends up asserting that capability may best be measured as a product of population and per capita productivity, i.e., gross national product (pp. 208-15). If this model was the correct one, we would expect to see the strongest direct relationship between industrial mobility and war, and of course this is the case.

Second, the transition model appears more in agreement with the observed pattern of time lags. Since any national "challenger" to the dominant coalition in the international system will presumably begin its rise from a position of considerable relative inferiority, a long period of differential growth will be required before such a nation can constitute any conceivable threat to the current "topdog." This would imply that there might be a considerable time lag between the first observed increase in mobility and the onset of international war, and, again, this squares with the findings.

However, we cannot conclude from this relatively good fit that this model provides a completely satisfactory explanation of our results, for two reasons. First, as Organski formulates the model, it does not apply to the status relationships between and among *all* nations. It refers primarily to the situation in which the nation at the very top of the pecking order is challenged by the second-rank nation or a coalition of lower-ranking nations, although it can sometimes be applied as well to a situation in which the second-ranked power is challenged by the third in the hierarchy, as in the case of the Sino-Soviet dispute. It is not, however, intended to apply to the relations among lower-ranked members, since Organski apparently believes that their behavior is governed more by their relationships with the dominant nation and current "challenger" than by their own relative capabilities (pp. 367-71). Thus, even if the model is applicable to wars among the largest powers, it cannot account for the relationship between differential industrial mobility and war for the system as a whole unless it is generalized to include the status relationships amongst the nations in the middle or lower ranges of the status continuum.

Second, although the existence of a relationship between differential status mobility and war is a necessary precondition of the power transition hypothesis, it is not by itself a *sufficient* demonstration of the validity of the model. This is so because differences in rates of industrial growth may result not only in the *narrowing* of gaps between and among nations, but also in the *widening* of such differences. During much of the 140-year period under study, the nations which have experienced the highest rates of economic growth have been those already at or near the top of the status hierarchy (Lagos, 1963, pp. 10-11), leading one to suspect that differential industrial growth might have had more of a consolidating than an upsetting effect on the international pecking order. If this proved to be the case, of course, the power transition model would not explain the results.

Thus, while we cannot rule out the power transition interpretation of the connection between differential industrial growth and war, it cannot be definitely confirmed without further tests which would measure the degree of "passing" among rank-positions caused by differential growth.

The Economic Imperialism Model

The final model that shall be considered here is what has generally come to be termed the economic imperialism hypothesis of international war. As noted in Chapter 5, industrial growth may lead in many nations to considerable pressures for new markets, opportunities for investment, raw materials, and so forth. When the rates of economic growth are very uneven, with some nations forging ahead while others lag behind, it is almost inevitable that these pressures will lead to a process of economic expansion by the faster-growing nations into those areas of the world with less industrial, more stagnant economies (Hobson, 1938; Waltz, 1959, pp. 145-56).

This expansion can easily lead to war in several different ways. First, in seeking to extend and consolidate their economic advantage in areas of the world with regimes that are politically unstable, or are not organized into nation-states, the more rapidly growing members of the system may fight to extend political control; illustrative cases are the European colonization of South and South East Asia and Africa. Second, such nations may fight to gain economic concessions from other sovereign states, as for example in the Sino-French, Anglo-Persian, or Sino-Japanese wars. Third, they may fight to secure economic dependencies belonging to less rapidly growing system-members, as in the Spanish-American war.

As with the power transition model, the economic imperialism model gives a reasonably good fit with some of the observed results. Since the model is based on economic growth, we would expect the strongest direct relationship between *industrial* mobility and war, and such is the case. Moreover, since according to this hypothesis political and military conflict would only follow an extended period of economic penetration, one might predict a considerable lag between such differential industrial growth and the onset of war, and this is indeed the finding.

This good fit does not mean, of course, that the economic imperialism model is without drawbacks as an explanation. First, it would appear to be at odds with at least one other feature of the results. Since 1825, the majority of wars allegedly waged for reasons of economic expansion, as well as virtually all the colonial and imperial (extrasystemic) wars, were fought during the nineteenth century. If the economic imperialism model were the correct one, we might therefore expect that the relationship between differential industrial growth and war would be stronger in the earlier than in the later part of the temporal domain. In fact, we find precisely the reverse: for the 1825-1919 period, the strength of the relationship is *below* that for the 140-year period as a whole; for the 1850-1964 period, the observed association is *above* that for the entire period.

Second, just as in the case of the other two models, it is not at all clear whether a relationship between differential industrial mobility and war constitutes sufficient evidence either to confirm or deny the hypothesis. It might be, for example, that economic expansion does not cause much conflict when only a limited number of nations are engaged in rapid industrialization and differential growth was high, since under these conditions there would be a relatively large "pie" to divide amongst a few (Rosecrance, 1963, pp. 232-67). If, however, *many* nations began to engage in rapid industrialization (and, as a consequence, *differential* industrial mobility was comparatively low), conflict might rapidly develop as the competition for markets, resources, and capital outlets became more intense and the pool of available resources scarcer. Wars of economic imperialism may therefore just as plausibly be associated with high *mean* growth, even if there are only small *differences* between national growth rates.

Thus, once again it would seem that any definitive statements about the applicability of the model will require further tests, in this case those relating particular configurations or "profiles" of industrial growth with the amount of war begun in the system.

Summary

There would seem to be a number of plausible models which could account for the observed direct connection between war and mobility on the industrial capability dimension. All have some difficulties; this may indicate that none of the explanations set forth above are adequate, or, perhaps, that there exists more than one causal sequence linking differential industrial mobility and war. At all events, none can be offered as more than tentative at this stage, requiring much additional evidence for conclusive demonstration. A common feature of this evidence is the need to move beyond simple summary indices of the distribution of capability change within the system as a whole to those which measure more complex configurations of system structure.

Having examined some possible explanations for the observed relationship between industrial mobility and war, let us now turn to examine the apparent causal connection between status inconsistency and the amount of war begun in the international system.

Status Inconsistency and War:
Alternative Models

On the face of it, the task of accounting for the strong and apparently nonspurious relationship between status inconsistency and war would be much easier than explaining the rather unexpected direct relationship between differential status mobility and war discussed above. The line of reasoning which has led many to suspect a connection between status inconsistency was carefully outlined in the first two chapters, and, given that the very positive findings would appear to confirm the hypothesis, one might suppose that the only remaining tasks are to draw the appropriate conclusions for future research and discuss the implications of the findings for the conduct of policy. Such, however, is not the case, for two reasons. First, as noted in earlier discussion, the original model is by no means the *only* plausible causal sequence which could account for the observed relationship between status inconsistency and war. Second, there are some features of the results which might lead to an alternative interpretation of the findings. What follows, then, is a reexamination of the earlier model in light of the evidence, followed by some plausible alternatives suggested by the findings, and concluding with an evaluation of their relative probabilities and suggestions for further research which might provide more definitive answers.

The Frustration-Aggression Model

Let us begin the discussion with a brief recapitulation of the model outlined in Chapter 2. There it was argued that a nation (or, more accurately, national decision-makers and their attentive publics) will adjust status expectations to capability. If the status attributed to that nation by the other national actors in the system is lower than its self-perceived capability ranking, decision-makers and publics will believe this to be unjust and inequitable. In short, it is hypothesized that status inconsistency creates dissatisfaction because it violates the crucial system norm that nations receive rewards in proportion to their position on the capability pecking order. The frustration thus engendered, coupled with the leverage possessed by such a nation in having relatively high capability status, create both the motive and opportunity for increasingly aggressive international behavior. This may result in war if the discrepancy remains uncorrected.

To a very large extent, this model is compatible with the observed findings. To begin with, it accounts for the strong relationship observed between status inconsistency and war when *no* time lag was employed. If status inconsistency did not operate directly to stimulate hostile or aggressive attitudes on the part of national elites and their internal clientele, we would not expect to observe so strong a bivariate relationship except when a long time-lag was introduced.

Second, this model would explain why the apparent effect of status inconsistency on the amount of war begun in the system was greater when we examined the later portion of the temporal domain. If status inconsistency makes its impact by engendering a sense of frustration amongst those within a nation who perceive it, one might expect a greater influence on national behavior during the period in which a larger and more heterogeneous group of citizens were influential in the foreign policy process. Although there are, of course, enormous variations from nation to nation, for most nations in the system the size and influence of the attentive group increased sharply during the late nineteenth and early twentieth centuries.

Finally, as noted earlier, this model would explain why the particular *indices* of status inconsistency which predict best to war vary with the time period examined. If national elites and attentive publics were sensitive to discrepancies between perceived national capability and attributed status, then it might be expected that the indices of status inconsistency which predicted best to war would be those based on capability measures most closely corresponding to current beliefs about national power. Such appears to have been the case; with the exception of the iron and steel production index discussed above, we see a gradual shift in the nature of the indices which predict best to war, those which measure mere size (total population and number of military personnel) gradually giving way to those which are sensitive to a nation's sophistication and level of development (urban population and military expenditures). This shift could be interpreted as reflecting the growing awareness (engendered in part by contacts with large, non-European societies such as Turkey and China) that capability was based on far more than sheer size.

However, if this model fits well with most of the observed results, it does not accord so well with one crucial feature of the findings. Specifically, it does not explain why an even stronger relationship between status inconsistency and war was discovered when a ten to fifteen year time lag was employed. To be sure, by itself such a long time lag would not necessarily cast doubt on the validity of the model. It could be argued that many national decision-makers, at least in the pre-World War II era, were very slow to perceive and react to status changes within the system, being as always prisoners of inherited conventional wisdom; examples might be the surprise which greeted Japan's victory over Russia in 1905, and the equal astonishment which accompanied the sudden fall of France in 1940. Perceptions of national status inconsistency may likewise become apparent only very gradually, accounting for the long observed lag between the existence of status inconsistency and its culmination in the onset of war.

Unfortunately, if we choose to explain the existence of a strong lag effect in this way, we immediately run into two difficulties. First, it is difficult to see how we can have it both ways; if we assume that status perceptions change very slowly, we can no longer explain the existence of a relationship when no time lag is employed. Second, we can no longer account so well for the observed differences in the particular *indices* of status inconsistency which predict well to war in the different time periods; it is scarcely probable that national decision-makers will be very *slow* to react to important changes in the international pecking order while at the same time very *quick* to respond to changes in the national attributes which go to make up this rank-ordering.

On balance, then, while the "frustration-aggression" model may *partly* account for the findings, it does not appear to be a wholly satisfactory explanation. Let us, then, see to what extent other possible models could better account for the observed results.

The Status Confusion Model

One possible alternative line of reasoning would stress the possibilities for confusion and judgmental error which might attend status discrepancies in the international system. This argument would run as follows. A common feature of several popular models of the international system is the emphasis they place on a decision-maker's ability to estimate accurately the capabilities and status position of other nations vis-à-vis one's own. In the balance of power model, such finely tuned perceptions—particularly with regard to military capability— are vital if statesmen are to react quickly enough to counteract potential threats to the balance (Gulick, 1955, pp. 24-9). In the power transition model, misperceptions about capability status on the part of the "challenger" can lead him to initiate hostilities in the mistaken belief that he can overturn the established order (Organski, 1968, pp. 371-3).

If such confusion and misperception about status represent an important source of danger to peace and stability in the system, it is easy to see how status inconsistency may generate such misperceptions. Even the most sagacious statesman will be influenced to some extent in his evaluation of a nation's capability by the judgments of his counterparts in other nations. If the collective judgment of the comity of nations concerning the *importance* of a given national actor—what we have termed the attributed status of a nation—is seriously at variance with its *capabilities*, errors in evaluating these capabilities would undoubtedly be greater in magnitude and more frequent in occurrence. Recent examples of such distorted evaluations due to status inconsistency might be the serious underrating of Soviet capabilities prior to the launch of Sputnik, and the similar misestimate of Chinese capabilities prior to the explosion of that nation's first atomic device.

To some extent, this model fits quite well with the observed results. First, it accounts well for the existence of a relationship when no time lag is employed, since presumably any confusion generated by status inconsistency will tend to dissipate with time as decision-makers receive feed-back concerning their evaluations. Second, it accounts even better than the previous model for the observed variations in the particular indices of status inconsistency which predict best to war in different time periods; according to this model, what is important are the discrepancies between attributed status on the one hand and real, not perceived, capability on the other. It might therefore be expected that the results would be quite sensitive to overtime changes in the attributes which comprise a nation's power base. Finally, this model is congruent with results in a still more attractive sense: since it is compatible with both the balance of power and power transition models which were advanced as possible explanations of the observed *direct* relationship between differential status mobility and war, it leaves open the intriguing possibility that one of these or perhaps some similar model might be capable of explaining *both* of the major patterns in our findings.

There are, however, two important drawbacks to this "confusion" model linking status inconsistency and war. First, for precisely the reason it offers a good explanation for the existence of a relationship in the no-lag case, it would appear unable to account for the relationship observed with a very long lag; after ten or fifteen years, any confusion in evaluating national capability generated by status inconsistency should have lessened, not grown stronger. Second, and more important, it is basically at odds with still another finding. If status inconsistency led to conflict by creating confusion regarding national capabilities, we would expect that discrepancies between the basic dimensions of national capability *themselves* (demographic, military, and industrial) would prove to exercise a strong influence on war, since (even more than discrepancies between the various capability indices and *attributed* status), such inconsistencies would make difficult the evaluation of national capability. This, however, did not prove to be the case; in pretests the relationship between these discrepancies and war was found to be virtually nil.

In short, then, the status confusion model does not seem to do any better, and in some respects fares rather worse than the original. While later evidence may demonstrate the contrary, on the basis of the present findings it can scarcely be considered a strong alternative.

The Arms Race Model

A second alternative model may be constructed which represents only a slight modification of the original "frustration-aggression" approach, yet which, in some respects, gives a better fit. According to this line of reasoning, status inconsistency does indeed exercise a frustrating and disturbing influence on a nation, but it is unlikely that in all cases this will result immediately in overtly aggressive behavior. It is more probable that a nation will first attempt to redress the perceived injustice by putting pressure of one sort or another on the member or members of the international system held responsible for the low attributed status. Given the mores of the international system, such pressure will no doubt often involve at least a show of military force, and, in order to exert it, the aggrieved nation may embark upon a program of military expansion.

Moreover, it is possible that status discrepancies may induce such expansion in another way. If a nation's military capability should drop below the other dimensions in its status set, and if it has the industrial and demographic capability to rectify the situation, the inconsistent nation may embark upon a rapid military build-up to balance its rankings. In either case, if other nations have reason to feel threatened by such an expansion, an arms race is not an improbable outcome, and, of course, the explosive properties of such self-feeding spirals of military might have been amply illustrated in the history of the international system (Singer, 1958).

This model fits the findings well in certain key respects. First, it would easily account for the ten to fifteen year time-lag which must be introduced to optimize the status inconsistency-war relationship; not only is there likely to be a lag between the perception of status inconsistency and the launching of an arms-backed foreign policy drive to rectify it, but there may be a further delay before such a posture provokes an arms race, and an additional lapse of time before the arms race becomes sufficiently serious to result in war. Second, it would appear to account well for the observed increase in the relationship over time. In the age of advanced weaponry an arms race is likely to produce a greater increase in the magnitude and severity of war than when the implements of war are relatively primitive. Third, it would account for the decrease in the optimal time-lag from the earlier to the later portion of the temporal domain. Presumably, both the genesis and the process of an arms race are likely to proceed with greater rapidity in an era when weapons become obsolete more rapidly. Finally, and most important, there is some direct empirical evidence to give credence to this model. In a preliminary path analysis of seven factors linked with war onset, it was discovered that status inconsistency increased the likelihood of war to a large extent (although by no means exclusively) as a result of its tendency to augment global arms levels (Wallace, 1972).

But despite this good fit, the arms race model is not without liabilities as an explanation of war. First, the indices of status inconsistency which are most closely related to war do not correspond to the predictions we would make from this model. If the arms race hypothesis were the correct one, we would expect that inconsistencies between *military* capability and attributed status would be the best predictors. While indices of inconsistency based on military capability generally predict well, they are the best predictors only in the 1850-1964 period using a ten-year lag, and, furthermore, they do not tend to make as important a contribution to the total variance in the amount of war explained as do indices based on other dimensions of capability. Second, while this model explains the existence of a relationship with a long lag, it cannot account for the no-lag results, as even in the nuclear age a near instantaneous arms race is hardly likely.

Finally, if this was indeed the correct explanation for the observed connection between status inconsistency and war, one might expect the onset of war to be preceded by the rapid buildup of military activity on the part of the nations involved. This should result in a strong *direct* relationship between differential rate of change on military capability and war, with very little lag. As can be seen from Tables 4-2 and 4-4, however, we do not observe such a relationship. Thus while the arms race model, unlike the previous ones discussed, can adequately account for the ten to fifteen year lagged relationship, it is by no means a complete explanation for the observed findings.

The Alliance Model

Up until now, the models put forward have dwelled more or less exclusively on the *direct* effects of status inconsistency on the behavior of nation-states. Such discrepancies, however, may conceivably act to increase the magnitude and severity of war in quite a different way: they may alter the patterns of formal or informal affiliation and interaction in the international system, and these changed structural configurations may be more war-prone than those they replace. One structural configuration which may play this role is the pattern of alliances between and among the members of the system.

If we assume that status inconsistency does indeed put discomforting pressures on a nation, it will of course seek changes in those aspects of the international status quo which are understood to be at the root of the discrepancy. But it is doubtful that unilateral action of a warlike nature would always be the first method employed to achieve the necessary changes, except perhaps in the case of international "pariahs" which do not have the normal opportunities for relationships with other nations. In most cases, a better strategy will be to attempt such changes by acting in concert with other nations:

States (struggle) for what they regard as appropriate places in the distribution of power . . . (by the) "artificial" method of linking themselves to the strength of other states. Indeed, this is the only method available to the bulk of states in the actual circumstances of modern history (Claude, 1963, p. 89).

In other words, we might suppose that a high level of status inconsistency in the international system will result in an increased level of alliance activity directed towards altering the status quo. Another line of reasoning leading us to the same hypothesis is suggested by the theory of coalition formation. Since the problem facing a status inconsistent nation may be viewed as that of obtaining certain types of outcomes which are consistent with its capabilities, one would expect national decision-makers to seek new interaction opportunities which produce such outcomes. Russett (1968) has suggested that, as a working hypothesis, it is not unreasonable to assume that the distribution of payoffs within an alliance will be some function of the capabilities of the partners. If so, it might be supposed that another attraction of alliances for status inconsistent nations would be that the alliance bond would result in an upgrading of ascribed status *within* the framework of the alliance, as well as assisting the nation in achieving higher status in the system as a whole. One might expect further that such coalitions would stimulate the formation of defensive pacts or agreements on the part of those whose interests are threatened by such activity. The combination of these two mutually reinforcing tendencies should result in an increase in the proportion of nations entering into alliance bonds.

The reader has no doubt anticipated that this causal chain may readily be extended directly to the onset of war. International relations scholars are by no means in agreement over whether alliance bonds tend to diminish the level of war by reducing the temptations for potential aggressors, or augment it by polarizing conflict in the system, but the empirical evidence indicates that the overall relationship is positive, though weak and probably nonadditive (Singer and Small, 1968). This suggests the possibility of a two-stage causal link between status inconsistency and war via alliance aggregation.

For several reasons the alliance model would appear an attractive explanation of the lagged relationship between status inconsistency and war. As noted by Singer and Small, the relationship between alliance aggregation and war is optimized only when a three-year time lag is introduced. Since it would no doubt be some time before status inconsistency resulted in the creation of formal alliances, a ten to fifteen year time lag for the two-step sequence is scarcely surprising. Moreover, there is some empirical evidence to support the model; path analysis shows that alliance aggregation is a significant—albeit not the most important—link between status inconsistency and war. But it would be well not to make too much of this finding, however, as a closer look at the Singer-Small results raises important difficulties.

First, while they found a *positive* relationship between alliance aggregation and war in the twentieth century, Singer and Small discovered that the relationship in the nineteenth century is *negative*. If the primary effect of status inconsistency was to increase alliance aggregation, it might be expected that the status inconsistency-war relationship for the earlier period would be negative or vanishing. While it is somewhat lower for the 1825-1919 period than for the temporal domain as a whole, it is still quite strong and positive.

Second, if alliance aggregation were the sole, or even the primary intervening link between status inconsistency and war, we would predict that the observed association between alliance aggregation and war would be greater than that between status inconsistency and war. Such, however, is not the case; even with no time lag, the observed association between status inconsistency and war is considerably the larger, and this difference is accentuated if a longer time-lag is employed. Thus, while alliance aggregation may form part of one causal sequence linking status inconsistency and war, the alliance model is evidently not a *sufficient* explanation for the findings.

The Intergovernmental Organization Model

Another way in which status inconsistency may act on the structure of the international system to increase the likelihood of war is by affecting the institutional structure designed to reduce the level of conflict within the system; status inconsistency may well seriously interfere with the formation and functioning of intergovernmental organizations. If the reasoning set forth thus far is correct, status inconsistency will both increase tensions and result in a greater degree of stress being placed on the competitive aspects of the relationships between nations. In such an atmosphere, major initiatives of a cooperative nature between nations will be relatively less frequent. One would expect this to be especially true of those acts of cooperation which imply formal, long-term commitments at a time when the status quo is under attack. Indeed, a continuing theme in the history of many international organizations has been the assaults made upon them by "revisionist" nations. In other words, status inconsistency is likely to have a strong negative impact on the creation, development and functioning of international organizations, regardless of whether they are oriented towards political objectives or are designed to fulfill a purely technical role. And if, as most of us believe, the existence of such organizations does in some way help to reduce the likelihood of international war, we may hypothesize the existence of a causal link based on the tendency of status inconsistency to inhibit the growth of organizations which serve to promote cooperation and reduce tension in the international system.

Like the previous model, the intergovernmental organization hypothesis would account for the long time lag required to optimize the status inconsistency-war relationship. On the whole, however, it is even less satisfactory than the alliance model as an explanation of the results, for two reasons. First, while intergovernmental organizations have become increasingly associated with efforts to prevent war and promote international cooperation in the twentieth century, it is highly unlikely that they were either numerous or strong enough to play such a role in the nineteenth. As noted by Wallace and Singer (1970), it was not until 1885 that there were more than a dozen intergovernmental organizations, and by the end of the First World War they still numbered no more than forty-one. Thus, even if the intergovernmental organization hypothesis could explain the findings for the 1850-1964 period, it could scarcely account for the existence of strong relationship between status inconsistency and war for the 1825-1919 period.

A second and more damaging criticism is that the model is only partially in accord with the existing systematic evidence about the relationship between intergovernmental organization and war. Singer and Wallace (1970) have shown that for the 1820-1964 period as a whole there appears to be virtually no association between the amount of interstate war begun and either the amount of intergovernmental organization *extant* in the previous five and ten years, or the amount *established* during these periods of time. Wallace (1972) found that the amount of IGO created in the previous five-year period did exercise an *indirect* impact on war by helping to reduce global arms levels, but there was no direct link between the two variables. While of course the amount of such organization may be only a crude indicator of its impact and effectiveness, these findings would appear to effectively rule out the intergovernmental organization model, at least for the present.

An Evaluation

Having examined in some detail a number of different alternative models which would explain the patterns and trends in the findings, it appears difficult to draw anything but the most ambivalent and tentative conclusions. On the one hand, we saw that the status inconsistency model as originally formulated was by itself inadequate to account for *all* the observed findings. On the other hand, the various alternative models scarcely fared any better, and in many cases appeared to be far less satisfactory than the original both in accounting for the findings of this study and in meshing them with the systematic evidence already obtained. One possible inference we may draw from this, of course, is that some entirely different explanation is needed to account for the results; given the paucity of hard evidence in this area, and the tentative and incomplete character of the study, we are in no position to rule out such an interpretation. It may well be that further research will enable the construction of a more adequate theoretical model.

An alternative conclusion is equally plausible, however. It may be that status inconsistency and war are linked by not one, but several different causal sequences. It might be, for example, that status inconsistency acts both *directly* to increase aggressive national behavior by stimulating national frustration, while at the same time acting to increase the probability of war *indirectly* by stimulating arms races or by altering some aspect of the structure of the international system such as its alliance configurations. Assuming a multiplicity of causal sequences permits us to account for the existence of a strong status inconsistency-war relationship both with and without a time lag. Moreover, such an interpretation of our findings accords more nearly with our intuitive belief that the onset of war involves not a single sequence of processes, conditions, and behaviors, but the overlap and confluence of many. Preliminary tests suggest that this explanation is indeed the correct one (Wallace, 1972), and it is to be hoped that the various lines of reasoning advanced here may point to the next steps for further research in this area.

Some Overall Conclusions on Interpretation

It is difficult to summarize briefly the diverse and often conflicting interpretations which may be given the findings produced by this study. Nor is it easy to come to any definitive conclusions concerning which, if any, of the various models outlined represent the most acceptable explanations of these findings. Throughout the chapter, however, two basic themes have continually recurred, and it might be well to restate and emphasize them prior to discussing the policy implications of the findings.

First, although this study began as the test of a relatively straightforward hypothesis derived from social psychology, as the results were examined closely it became increasingly clear that the relationships discovered between and among the various indices were indicative of anything but a clear-cut set of answers to the questions posed at the outset. We saw that only by making the most farfetched assumptions or relying on very implausible inferences was it possible to subsume all the findings under a single, simple explanatory rubric. In other words, although the magnitude of the various correlation and dependence coefficients, and the explanatory power of the regression equations, all indicate that there are indeed strong relationships between war and both status inconsistency and differential status mobility, this is far from writing finis to the matter. Rather, it merely raises new and more challenging questions about the whole conception of status in the international system and its relation to war.

A second recurrent theme has been the extent to which the findings here touch upon other models, beliefs, evidence, and theoretical propositions current in the international relations literature. We saw how the present findings could be linked with the balance of power and power transition models, economic imperialism, the attitudes of decision-makers, configurations of alliance bonds, and the origin and operation of intergovernmental organizations. Given the strength of the relationships found in this study, it may well turn out that an understanding of a wide variety of phenomena in the international system will depend upon a knowledge of the effects of status relationships between and among nations.

The unifying link between these two themes—the obvious complexity of the effects of status in the international system and the pivotal role which it may well play in the structure of and relationships within that system—is the need for further research. As was mentioned time and again both in this chapter and the one preceding it, there are almost an endless variety of ways in which additional studies could improve, confirm, qualify, or develop the findings that have been presented here. Given the tremendous importance of the task of accounting for the frequency, magnitude, and severity of war in the international system, and the evident contribution which the study of international status relationships can make to that task, it is scarcely too much to hope that some of these opportunities may be pursued.

7

Practical Applications

Introduction

Whatever the merits of this study as a piece of scientific research, it is not only in this role that it must be judged. Implicit in the rationale of this and all research into the causes of war is the urgent need to generate knoledge which will provide at least some minimal assistance in reducing the continuing global carnage. In this chapter, we will attempt to determine what guidelines for policy—if any—may be gleaned from the findings, and what difficulties might be encountered in acting upon them.

Now there are those who would deny the utility—even the legitimacy—of such a quest right from the outset (Bleicher, 1970). According to this view, our knowledge of the international system is so rudimentary and incomplete that we should be extremely wary of using these findings as a guide in any realm of action. For one thing, what have been produced here—as in most systematic studies in the field—are merely empirical generalizations. To apply these to specific situations involves making such enormous inferential leaps, and ignoring such a wide variety of possible confounding influences, that the result will be little more than guesswork. Worse yet, it is argued, the limited reliability of such statistical regularities combined with the complexity of the phenomena involved may result in our efforts making things worse. One need only point to early efforts to reduce automobile emissions in California—which in fact may have aggravated the smog problem—to demonstrate that even very sophisticated applied science may produce unwelcome results.

While those who make these arguments are correct to point out the limitations of our current knowledge, to deny the results any practical utility on this basis is a misapplication of scientific caution, in two respects. First, the fact that our findings are "merely" empirical generalizations does not necessarily detract from their usefulness. It is important to remember that concepts, generalizations, and findings which are only partially satisfactory from the point of view of scientific theory may be entirely adequate to deal with some specific practical problems (A. Kaplan, 1964, p. 404). A powerful illustration of this is to be found in the great Gothic cathedrals of Europe. The builders of these structures were possessed of only the crudest of theoretical tools; they did not know how to calculate the mass of a body from its measurements, and it would be two centuries before anyone in Europe systematically distinguished the geometric center of an object from its center of gravity. That such impressive monuments could be built even without such supposedly "fundamental" architectural concepts ought to be a salutory reminder that the lack of a deductive paradigm is not always the barrier that we suppose.

Second, to argue that reliability problems preclude applying the findings is equally misleading. For short-run policy purposes, the probability that one's inferences might be in error is not by itself the crucial factor; what is important is their reliability *compared to* competing sources of evidence, propositions, and hypotheses. Since the greater part of the information and generalizations arising from the scholarship and practice of international politics is neither data-based, nor rigorous, nor often even well-articulated, it is simply irresponsible to claim that the results of scientific research in the field should have no role in guiding policy. Of course our findings are never as good as they might be; the point is that they are usually better than the conventional wisdom. For the future we can always hedge our bets with more research; for now, as policy makers and activists never tire of telling us, that is a luxury we cannot afford.

Before proceeding let us reemphasize that the suggestions put forward here are necessarily somewhat (although by no means wholly) speculative. Moreover, they are—again of necessity—in the nature of broad guidelines and frameworks within which policy can be developed rather than specific policy recommendations. Nevertheless, it is to be hoped that they will prove useful, if only to initiate debate on so vital a subject.

Specific Problems of Application

Even if in the general case we can justify the translation of first-pass empirical findings into policy guidelines, there are several features of this particular study which pose additional problems. First and foremost, there is the stumbling block alluded to in Chapter 2; since the relationships among status inconsistency, mobility, and war are examined only at the level of the international system as a whole, and since these relationships may not hold at the national level, how is it possible to derive guidelines for specific nation-states?

To answer this objection it is necessary to specify our policy goal more precisely. If it were our aim to advise states how to minimize their *own* involvement in war, the findings produced in this study would indeed be inapplicable. But if the question is how to minimize *global* violence, this problem does not arise, as we are not seeking to infer causal relationships about the likelihood of conflict involving any *particular* state or group of states. It is perfectly legitimate to suggest ways in which nations—or indeed any other social coalition or group—might direct their actions so as to reduce global levels of status inconsistency and status mobility, or alternatively to dampen the impact of these variables on the level of war in the system as a whole. Although some nations may be too preoccupied with regional problems to spare much time for such wide-ranging concerns, the growing awareness of global interdependence cannot but insure us a clientele.

A second problem arises from the length of the historical period examined. While an extensive temporal domain enhances the power of one's findings, it raises an obvious question of relevance when attempting to use the findings to shed light on contemporary problems. Are findings based to a large extent on data from the pre-World War I international system a reliable guide for the 1970s? Obviously a definitive answer cannot be given at the present state of our knowledge, but there are certainly no grounds for dismissing our results out of hand. As was hypothesized in Chapter 1, and partially confirmed in Chapter 4, sensitivity to national status position may well be one of the most durable elements in the relationship between structure and behavior in the international system. In fact, we shall argue below that this relationship is unlikely to be seriously affected by anything short of a major change in the structural characteristics of the system itself.

A final problem concerns our very limited knowledge of the key intervening variables which generate and mediate the impact of status mobility and inconsistency. Without such additional information, it would seem difficult to present even rough guidelines for policy. But in fact the picture is not quite as bleak as it seems at first glance. As we shall see, we can account fairly well for the major changes in our independent variables with the aid of economics, and some information about the variables mediating their impact on war is already available. Thus our present knowledge should prove sufficient to support the very tentative conclusions set forth below.

The Control of Status Mobility and Inconsistency

The most obvious implication to emerge from our results is the need to control global levels of status mobility and inconsistency if international conflict is to be held to acceptable levels. But precisely how is this to be done? Neither of the two most obvious answers seem either plausible or attractive.

The Manipulation of Attributed Status

The first and most obvious procedure would be to increase the level of recognition, benefits, and prestige accorded by the system to those nations whose attributed status is markedly lower than their national capability, i.e., adjusting attributed status to status expectations. In this way it might be possible to halt or check any animosities or war-generating sequence of events that may have been set in motion. However, there would appear to be four important disadvantages to this strategy.

To begin with, changes in the attributed status of a nation almost always requires the consent of at least several major powers and their allies. If—as is frequently the case—the "upwardly mobile" nation has incurred the wrath of many of the world's major nations, the chances for an early adjustment of the pecking order will be slim.

A second difficulty makes the prospects for such timely status adjustments even less likely. As mentioned earlier, reputational status is almost inevitably a constant-sum attribute, meaning that every national gain must be balanced by someone else's loss. Obviously any "reapportionment" would not be readily accepted by those on the losing side of the equation. Such a redistribution might still take place if the larger powers, secure in *their* status and aware of the dangers of inconsistency, were to act so as to promote status equilibration. But all too often the "losers" will be clients or allies of these same major powers, reducing the likelihood of a concerted initiative for change.

A third objection to this course of action is an ethical one. By granting attributed status (and the rewards which accompany it) on the basis of capability, we would be overlooking the fact that there are often very pressing ethical reasons for *not* granting such status. The clearest examples are those nations which are governed by regimes which practice totally abhorrent and morally unacceptable policies within their borders, such as Nazi Germany and South Africa. In such cases, the danger of war which may result from withholding attributed status must surely be balanced against the great harm that may be caused by lending support and sanction to such regimes.

A fourth and final difficulty lies in the fact that the adoption of status manipulation as a peace strategy means the overt acceptance of the principle of *de jure* national inequality. This runs up against one of the most cherished beliefs held by the leaders of nations and international organizations alike: that the sovereign equality of nations is a good in and of itself, and constitutes the basis for a sound international order (Lagos, 1963, pp. 22-3). Moreover, a large measure of equality in relations among nations in the international system has been regarded not only as intrinsically good, but as more conducive to peace than a situation in which the rewards and honors bestowed by the system are closely controlled by those at the top of a well-defined hierarchy. The founders of the League of Nations went so far as to define peace as virtually equivalent to the rights of small nations, and it seems clear that the same assumption undergirds much of the philosophy and operation of the United Nations system as well (Nicholas, 1963, pp. 35-7). Thus, the implementation of a status equilibration strategy would inevitably meet great resistance from the very organizational leadership most committed to a search for international peace, and, as a consequence, the prospect of initiating and implementing such a strategy through world organizations does not appear very promising.

The Manipulation of Capability Status

The second obvious strategy for dealing with status inconsistency would be to reduce or eliminate the differences in rates of capability change. As we saw, such differential changes were in large measure responsible for generating status inconsistency and, in some cases, exercised a strong independent influence on war by themselves. Thus, by "smoothing out" the differences in national growth rates it might be possible to lessen the risk of war. But clearly, the disadvantages of the status equilibration strategy pale beside the drawbacks that would be encountered in any attempt to manipulate national capability.

First and most obviously, it is virtually impossible to conceive how such a manipulation could, in fact, be successfully undertaken. Some of the factors to be regulated, such as population growth and economic expansion, have usually proved difficult or impossible to adjust either upwards or downwards even when a major policy initiative is undertaken *within* a nation. The likelihood that such a manipulation can be undertaken successfully from the outside—possibly with the active opposition of the national leadership—would seem virtually nil. With regard to *military* capability, decades of fruitless disarmament talks have shown the difficulties of manipulating that dimension of national status.

Second, the strategy of equalizing rates of capability change has a fatal political and ethical drawback in that it would deny relative mobility and thus, in effect, freeze the status quo amongst nations. Such a solution would, of course, be acceptable to the superpowers (and indeed, there are many who would accuse them of planning towards such an eventuality), but it is almost certain to be unacceptable to those on the bottom of the existing pecking order. Moreover, it will be *least* acceptable to those to whom it must need be most quickly applied: the rapidly upwardly mobile.

Finally, even if it could be applied, such a strategy would produce grotesque and almost certainly unacceptable results *within* the various national societies, particularly on the economic dimension. This is an almost inevitable consequence of the vast *absolute* disparities in the levels of economic development between and among nations. On the one hand, for the nations at the bottom of the ladder, a relatively *high* rate of economic growth is a vital necessity to achieve acceptable standards of material well-being. On the other hand, the developed nations are becoming increasingly aware of the need for a *lower* rate of economic growth as an urgent prerequisite for the protection of the physical environment. Clearly, these needs would seem to rule out any uniform, stabilized global rate of growth in the near future, and with it the likelihood of controlling differential status mobility in the international system.

Some Alternative Policy Directions

At first blush, it would seem that the policy insights generated from our findings have succeeded less in finding a solution to the problem of war than in illuminating with still greater clarity the intractability of the situation. But before abandoning hope, let us recall that none of the models discussed in Chapter 6 hypothesized a direct link between our independent and dependent variables; in every case, some sequence of intervening variables was assumed to come into play. If it were possible to alter the values of the variables at some point in this sequence, the level of international war might be reduced even if status cannot be effectively controlled. Let us now turn to a very brief examination of some of the possibilities raised by the intervening processes already discussed.

Alliance Aggregation and Polarization

It was suggested earlier that high levels of status mobility and inconsistency would be likely to lead to the growth and polarization of military alliance groupings; the resulting tightly bonded, polarized system is more conducive to both the initiation and escalation of war. Would it be possible to intervene in this sequence by taking measures to reduce the formation and polarization of alliances under the pressure of status inconsistency and mobility? In particular, would it be possible to persuade policy-makers to loosen or shift their alliance ties if it could be demonstrated that the consequent reduction in polarization would decrease the likelihood of war?

At first sight this form of intervention would appear much easier than any attempt to alter the levels of our primary independent variables. Alliance formation, unlike status mobility, is directly manipulable by the policy process; moreover, in contrast to status inconsistency, the number and configuration of the military alliance patterns in the system can be markedly altered by the actions of a few large and medium-sized states (Wallace, 1973).

Upon closer inspection, however, this avenue does not appear quite so promising. For one thing, a large number of nations in the contemporary world do not have any real latitude in their choice of alliance memberships; if the local great power considers a nation within its sphere of influence, a change in military alignment—indeed, even the possibility of change—will bring severe sanctions, military confrontation, or even armed invasion. Moreover, most alliance ties have as their basis a real or perceived need to increase national security against a possible military enemy. However convincing a case the social scientist may make against military combinations as a threat to world peace, an individual nation is likely to perceive the alternatives somewhat differently; either join an alliance and obtain outside help in achieving the desired level of military strength, or fail to do so and accept the risk—or perhaps even the certainty—of military defeat should war break out. It is obvious how most policy-makers will respond to these alternatives.

In other words, it may be that any substantial efforts at modifying national military alignment patterns will have to await the development of an international system in which the dominance of the great powers is not so all-encompassing, and the exigencies of military security not so overwhelming. But in such a world the probability of armed conflict is almost certain to be greatly reduced, so we end up with a "solution" which presupposes that which it intends to achieve. This is not to say, of course, that the modification of alliance patterns must be ruled out completely as a way to reduce the risk of war, but only that it does not seem promising as a first step. As we shall see presently, the picture improves considerably if efforts to break or shift military ties are undertaken *after* some different, prior intervention.

Arms Control and Disarmament

A second way in which high levels of status mobility and inconsistency might be rendered less dangerous concerns the level and rate of increase in armed might within the system. As we saw, there is fairly strong evidence that increases in the values of our status variables are likely to accelerate the rate at which nations convert their material resources into military capability, and there is even stronger evidence that such growth of armed might often results in a self-feeding spiral of competition for military supremacy, tension, and conflict. If the evidence for the existence of this causal chain could be marshalled and convincingly presented to policy-makers, it could be argued that they might be more willing to engage in measures to control arms levels. As a consequence, the tensions produced by status mobility and inconsistency might be less likely to issue in all out military hostilities.

But as with the other approaches discussed so far, there seems little likelihood that such efforts are by themselves likely to prove successful. As long as self-help buttressed by military alliances remains a nation's only reliable protection against external danger, disarmament is not likely to prove any more "salable" in the near future than it has been for the past two generations. Thus far, only reductions in tensions and the threat of war have had any major success in reducing the armed might of nations; indeed, the history of attempts at multilateral disarmament seems to suggest that durable agreement is only reached when the parties involved have largely rejected the option of resolving their differences by a resort to force. It would thus appear we are back where we started again; the precondition for a warless world is nothing less than the achievement of that world itself.

At this point the reader may complain that the discussion so far has been needlessly pessimistic, omitting those approaches which either have had some success or might conceivably prove effective if more effort were made to implement them. Why not, for example, examine the possible role of inter-governmental organization as a means of preventing tension-producing forces from leading to armed conflict?

Intergovernmental Organization

As mentioned in Chapter 6, intergovernmental organization has apparently played at least a minor role in the process connecting our independent variables to the onset of war. Status inconsistency and mobility seem to inhibit the creation and expansion of IGOs, and the resulting slower rate of growth—and, occasionally, decline—of these international institutions contributes at least indirectly to an increased probability of global conflict. Consequently, if policy makers were to increase their efforts towards international institutionalization independently of the levels of status-related hostility in the system, it is quite possible that the danger of war could be reduced somewhat.

But encouraging though this seems, such an approach poses the same problem discussed at length above with reference to alliance polarization and arms levels; will it be possible to encourage the establishment and growth of IGOs without waiting for improvements in other structural and behavior variables which affect the war-proneness of the international system? Many would answer in the negative, citing the overwhelmingly disappointing experiences with the League of Nations and the United Nations, and the inability of a multitude of special purpose IGOs to accomplish very much in terms of concrete international regulation. Even the functionalist claim that the growth of the scope and power of IGO can proceed in the face of international conflict (Mitrany, 1946) seems scarcely tenable in the light of post-World War II experience; despite the proliferation of intergovernmental bodies in this period, there is little or no evidence that they have had much independent impact on the conflict behavior of nations (Claude, 1971; Singer and Wallace, 1970). For the IGO approach to develop and take effect, there are at least two crucial prerequisites: the existence of large areas of common interest in those sectors of human activity where the development of IGO is to take place, and an ability to involve progressively larger clientele within each nation in the IGO's activities.

Thus, while an approach which seeks to regulate status-generated conflict by the construction and expansion of IGOs shows at least some promise, two other goals must be achieved in order to permit efforts in this direction to proceed smoothly. First, there must be at a minimum some limited success in reorienting national goals away from the zero-sum competition for international status and towards more cooperative forms of endeavor. Second, there must be some involvement of the major interest groups of the society—be these economic, religious, bureaucratic, or whatever—in the process of IGO growth. Both of these goals imply action undertaken in the *domestic* political process of the nations concerned, and it is to the modalities of such action that we now turn.

Salience Manipulation—A Possible Way Out?

As we have seen, virtually all of the plausible causal sequences linking status mobility and inconsistency with war take as their point of departure the sensitivity of national decision-makers, along with their domestic clientele and mass publics, to considerations of national status. If ways could be found to reduce this sensitivity and focus the attention of both decision-makers and publics in other directions—either towards domestic goals, or, better yet, towards active international cooperation—the tension-producing effects of inconsistencies and mobilities might be considerably reduced.

That such a strategy might work at least in principle is at least arguable from anecdotal evidence. During periods of severe domestic disorder or stress, policy elites have been forced by necessity to adopt what Wolfers has referred to as a strategy of "self-abnegation," and it has typically resulted in at least limited periods of peace despite high status inconsistency and mobility. An example might be the Soviet Union during the 1920s and '30s, forced by its internal circumstances to react less strongly than it otherwise might have to its very low attributed status. But, for obvious reasons, this case is not a very attractive model; avoiding external conflict at the expense of such massive internal violence surely represents little net gain, and, moreover, there is considerable evidence that large-scale domestic conflict sooner or later spills over into the international arena. The problem is, then, how to reduce the salience of status in a less sanguine, more controlled manner.

The Isolationist Solution

One possible solution would be to encourage the nation concerned to adopt a policy of more or less complete isolationism, withdrawing from international commitments and contacts and concentrating on the achievement of internal goals. This policy would be tension-reducing in two ways: first, by withdrawal the elite and attentive publics alike are spared the continuing frustration and pain of contacts which emphasize their nation's status discrepancy, and second, such frustration is not transmitted to the other nations of the international system as a possible source of conflict. Moreover, it may prove relatively easy to encourage some status inconsistent nations to adopt this kind of policy; a number of the writers cited in Chapter 2 have noted that withdrawal is often a more probable response than aggression in situations of status inconsistency.

But obviously this solution has at least two important drawbacks. To begin with, there are many nations whose geographic location or economic relationships virtually prohibit an isolationist policy. A nation surrounded by military enemies obviously cannot cut its ties to other friendly states except at peril of its survival, nor would such a policy be appropriate for a nation with an economy critically dependent on trade relationships. Needless to say, the more powerful and economically developed the nation, the less likelihood that an isolationist solution will be practicable. Moreover, whatever its practicability, the isolationist approach represents essentially a *negative* policy; it aims at preventing intercourse among nations where it may lead to conflict rather than redirecting it into more positive channels. Given the many other serious problems facing the contemporary world which must be solved collectively—especially the preservation of the biosphere—this hardly seems a satisfactory way to proceed.

Internal Transformation and Salience Reduction

So far the suggested remedies for the dangers posed by a world of rapid status mobility and high status inconsistency have been directed toward modifying the policies of existing governmental elites. As such they have been essentially incrementalist in cast; they have not assumed any fundamental changes in the goal structure or orientation of the present foreign policy decision makers. Those in command were assumed to be concerned primarily with their nation's material and psychic aggrandizement, and would react swiftly against any perceived threat to the privileges accruing from its standing in the global pecking order. We have seen that the prominent solutions put forward in the context of these elite values ran into severe difficulties. As long as nations can almost never be persuaded to take action which they perceive as compromising their military, economic, or prestige standing vis-à-vis others, the prospects for controlling the negative impact of status mobility and inconsistency would appear minimal.

But fortunately our quest for peace need not limit itself to the present policy-makers. The urgency of the task before us should not lead us to forget the tool most ready at hand is not always the most appropriate. If existing leaders are unlikely to take those steps which are necessary to prevent massive international violence, then the task of the concerned scholar should be to suggest changes in the composition of the policy-making group and how these might be effected (Wallace, 1971b).

Obviously this task is not an easy one. Simple replacement of existing personnel is not enough; as numerous governmental changes have demonstrated, the role constraints of policy-making jobs rapidly socialize all but the most inner-directed toward the value orientations of the previous occupant. To be at all effective, personnel change must be accompanied by a fairly extensive revision in the ideology or operating philosophy governing foreign policy decision-making; without the Labor Party's strong antiimperialist policy, for example, the switch from Churchill to Atlee would not have resulted in such "self-abnegatory" behavior as the withdrawal from India and the Eastern Mediterranean.

Moreover, there are many cases which seem to demonstrate that even the drastic alteration of personnel and ideology accompanying a major revolution may well be insufficient to produce more than a temporary remission of a nation's status seeking behavior. To return to the example of the Soviet Union, the initial concern of the revolutionary leadership with the world revolutionary struggle led them to almost total abandonment of Russian great power status at

Brest-Litovsk. But after the hope of world revolution had to be abandoned, it did not take long for Stalin to reverse this policy under the doctrine of "socialism in one country," effectively reasserting Russia's claim to a place in pecking order. Most scholars would argue that such was the inevitable result of self-abnegation carried out in isolation; it is only possible to abandon status seeking behavior if everyone else is willing to do so as well. In other words, such limited and anecdotal evidence as we possess suggests that if changes in the composition of national elites are to have any permanent influence in reducing the salience of national status position, they must be at once multilateral and involve fundamental changes in existing world views. It goes without saying that the probability of such a major transformation occurring in several important states at once must be considered rather small.

But the problem does not end here; nothing has been said about how this alteration in elite values is to occur in the first place. In states with authoritarian regimes the initiative—barring revolution—must come from within the ruling group itself, and most would argue that dissension resulting in major changes in orientation is rare in the absence of serious foreign policy reversals. Despite their more open systems, constitutional regimes often possess even more inertia in the field of foreign policy; the process of public participation serves more effectively as a means for the elite to mobilize support than as a method for altering the fundamental premises of foreign policy. Here again, only failure is likely to stimulate change, and when it does occur it is more likely to move the national stance toward aggression than toward abnegation.

But if the historical record of such attempts at foreign policy transformation has proven rather bleak, there are trends which may portend somewhat improved conditions for the future. For one thing, the explosive pace of technological change and its socio-economic aftermath in the post-World War II period—the growth of all-pervasive mass media, the establishment of consumer societies in the North Atlantic area, the increasing urbanization and industrialization of western, socialist, and Third World nations alike—have generated strong internal pressures in many nations for greater social and economic equality as well as for greater participation by non-elite groups in economic and political decision-making. These pressures are beginning to have two important results: first, they are increasingly requiring the diversion of resources from such status-related areas as military expenditures, foreign aid, and industrial investment to sectors which enhance the quality of life for the average citizen, such as public works, education, medical care, and environmental improvement; second, they are generating a growing realization in many segments of the mass public that status-seeking behavior in the international arena carries a heavy price in goods and services lost to the domestic sector. It may not be too much to hope that over the course of the next decade or so, these pressures might sharply reduce the degree to which foreign policy makers focus on their nation's position in the pecking order.

Of course this forecast may well turn out to be too optimistic. It is worth emphasizing, even at the cost of redundancy, that national elites are in most cases still capable of resisting erosion of their "latitudinal discretion" in foreign policy matters, and can usually prevent any challenge to the nation's basic foreign policy stance by invoking a real or imagined external threat, often coupled with accusations of domestic complicity or conspiracy. As long as a national elite enjoys an unchallenged monopoly of legitimate authority within its national boundaries, there can be no guarantee of any progress towards a lower level of status salience save its goodwill and enlightenment, and most would agree that this is a slender reed indeed. However, the same technological and socioeconomic changes that have led to a greater emphasis on domestic goals have also, as we shall see, considerably attenuated the Austinian sovereignty of most states. This fact should not only reduce resistance to a reorientation of national priorities, but opens up additional possibilities whereby the dangers of status mobility and inconsistency may be still further reduced. It is to these opportunities that we now turn.

The Ultimate Solution—Global Denationalization

In addition to creating pressures within states for the reordering of priorities, post-World War II technology and its socio-economic spinoff have considerably eroded internation barriers. Herz (1959) has shown how atomic technology has drastically increased the permeability of state borders from a military point of view; the development of mass media, the ever increasing importance of global trade and investment, and the growth of inexpensive international air transport networks have had a similar effect on civilian affairs. Let us cite a few examples. First, economic autarky has become impossible for even the largest and strongest of domestic economies, as the exigencies of trade, balance of payments and currency flows, and the growing scarcity of key raw materials dictate an ever greater degree of collective decision-making in the economic sector. Second, while cultural borrowing is as old as civilization, the new ease of travel and communication have so increased the international exchange of artifacts and patterns of behavior that it is now virtually impossible for any government to exercise any substantial control over changes in cultural patterns or social mores without resort to totalitarian expedients; the areas of popular music, academic governance, and sexual behavior provide ample illustration of this. Third, the greatly increased density of communication and transportation networks has meant that political and social unrest even in geographically and culturally remote areas of the world has had increasing impact on, and is of growing salience to, all nations in the global system; the Middle Eastern conflict has recently provided several striking examples of the permeability of national borders to civil and international conflict originating elsewhere. Last, but by no means least, the burgeoning role of multinational corporations has resulted in many important decisions concerning global investment and resource allocation being made quite outside the individual or even collective control of nation-states.

These and other similar changes all taken together have produced a gradual but persistent erosion of the sovereignty and legitimacy of individual nation-states. In the short run, of course, governments have often responded to this challenge with their timeworn authoritarian practices, so ably augmented by the same technology that gave rise to the problem. But by their very nature the difficulties these developments pose for national elites are not likely to be soluble by unilateral action. This leaves decision-makers with essentially two choices when confronted with this type of problem; they may either relinquish some measure of control over the subject in question, leaving the matter to be settled by the play of internal and transnational forces discussed above, or they may attempt to combine with other nations to reassert collective control. Different nations and circumstances have evoked different "mixes" of these two approaches. Generally, western nations have adopted the former solution in the area of private behavior. In the economic field the willingness to yield control has been noticeably less, with periods of laissez-faire being punctuated by attempts at collective control. And in dealing with the "spillover" of strife from other areas, the drive for concerted international action has been limited only by technical feasibility and the exigencies of global power politics.

For our purposes the important thing is that regardless of which approach is used, the result will be a reduction of the dangers inherent in movement and inconsistencies in the international pecking order. On the one hand, every area of human endeavor abandoned by the nation-state to subnational and trans-national groups or entities implies a lessening of concern for the well-being of the nation at the expense of a greater concern for other types of coalitions, resulting eventually in a reduction of the elite's ability to mobilize resources on behalf of national status position. On the other hand, as we have seen, every multilateral cooperative effort entered into has the potential to reduce or control the disturbing influence of interstate competition and rivalry, as well as building an institutional framework which can act as an agency of compensation and redress. If we assume that these two national responses to transnational disturbances proceed side by side, the result could be a transformed international system in which nation-states slowly gave ground on the one hand to a multiplicity of overlapping, crosscutting, and constantly shifting transnational groupings, and on the other to increasingly powerful and omnifunctional IGOs. In such a world order, status relationships among nations would drastically recede in importance and consequently in danger.

Of course there is no guarantee that national elites will respond to the growing challenge of intranational shifts in values and transnational penetration in either of these two "rational" ways. Instead they may respond to the crisis—as some nations already have—in a harsh, panic-stricken fashion, in the vain hope that ever more stringent measures against dissent and nonconformity coupled with an ever stronger external "defense posture" will be in itself sufficient to halt and reverse the erosion of their legitimacy. If this response predominates, the result would be something resembling the Orwellian antiutopia: totalitarian regimes reinforced by continual interstate violence presiding over stagnant economies and degenerate cultures. And even if this does not happen and the nation-state system gradually evolves into something less dangerous to species survival, it will not mean the millenium has arrived; there is nothing in the nature of either IGOs or transnational politics that precludes injustice, conflict, or even violence. But at least the problems so generated can be dealt with without the spectre of global annihilation or quasi-genocidal mass slaughter that is an ever-present possibility in the contemporary world.

International Status and the Concerned Individual: A Cautious Prescription

To sum up, our speculations have led us to identify two conditions under which the likelihood of international war might well be appreciably reduced: a shift in domestic priorities away from intense concern with national ranking and prestige, and a growth in non-governmental contacts among nations. We have also identified those social, economic, and political circumstances which seem likely to bring about such transformations. But discussing the possibilities for change in terms of organizations and collectivities leaves one last central question unanswered: how, if at all, can the *individual* who wishes a more peaceful world act so as to contribute to the desired end?

Obviously, the appropriate course of action will vary enormously with the particular circumstances of the person concerned, and thus it is scarcely feasible to offer detailed guidance here. But it *is* possible to outline, in a very general way, three roles in which an individual may reasonably hope to make a positive contribution.

The Advocate of Domestic Change

As we saw, the ability of contemporary states to engage in status-seeking behavior is critically dependent on their success in persuading mid-elites and attentive publics to identify themselves with the status goals of "their" nation. Consequently, the growing tendency for these groups to substitute goals based on the maximization of individual values represents an important check on one kind of war—provoking behavior. Efforts directed toward such goal-substitution, in addition to producing direct benefits for most members of the society, will have the important indirect side-effect of promoting peace.

From this it is clear that the role of peacemaker is open to concerned persons in many, if not most walks of life. It embraces not only those in formal and informal political roles engaged in the redirection of national priorities via the political system, but also those whose occupations bring them into contact with the processes whereby social values are shaped and administered; amongst others, educators, lawyers, social workers, and those working in the media seem particularly well-placed. To play their part, such professionals must of course abandon traditional conceptions of their roles as mere neutral transmitters, administrators, and arbiters of values originating elsewhere. Fortunately, such a strict construction of professionalism is already under strong attack in many societies, and the activist professional is increasingly the key role-model. If the members of these and other important occupational groups rededicate themselves to the furthering of individual values, and if this is coupled with widespread political action, the impact could well be substantial.

The International Citizen

Another conclusion stated that the development of transnational links among many different peoples in a wide variety of substantive areas was likely to attenuate further the ability of elites to focus attention on national status goals. Therefore, to the degree that a strong and extensive network of such ties can be built, the probability of war provoking national behavior will be that much reduced. Moreover, participation in the process of building such a net is open to others besides the skilled and educated; virtually any common interest, from astrophysics to acid rock, can serve as the basis for formal and informal ties linking people of many nations directly with one another. Once again, progress toward peace does not require that everyone engage in strenuous efforts outside the sphere of their normal activities, but rather that they direct some portion of these activities towards those with common interests in other societies as well as their own.

At this point it would be well to enter a major caveat. Certain transnational activities—particularly in the economic realm and specifically involving large corporations—have resulted in exploitation and the development of relationships of inequality between the international corporation and both governmental and nongovernmental groups in various "host" nations. Such one-sided relationships, far from curbing the deleterious effects of the international pecking order and thereby promoting peace, are likely to reinforce the very factors we have identified as being at the root of the problem. Whether the host government takes action against such corporations of its own volition, or whether it is driven to a firmer stance by political pressure from opposition groups, it will attempt to mobilize support for its policies by identifying the unequal and exploitative activities of such international corporations with their foreign origins. The result will be that transnational links of any type—even those undertaken on the basis of strict equality among those from different nations—are likely to be discredited and endangered. At the same time, such action gives a national elite yet another opportunity to confirm its stewardship of the national destiny and its role of protector of the masses against foreign danger, and also to emphasize collective identification with national goals as opposed to individual and particularistic ones. Such a result is precisely the opposite of that which we desire.

But this is not all. It is more than likely that the corporation's home government will take action to protect and further its economic interests wherever necessary. If—as is usually the case—the "home" nation possesses far more military might, much greater international influence, and substantially higher status than the "host" country, any action taken against the corporation abroad is likely to be interpreted as an affront to the former nation's position and privileges. The result is, more often than not, the application of some form of sanction against the "offending" nation, which in turn frequently results in a considerable degree of hostility and conflict between the two nations.

It would seem, then, that our unequivocal advocacy of increased transnational links requires qualification. Only such links as can be established *without exploitation or drastic inequality* are likely to have the beneficial effects hypothesized earlier. This probably rules out not only many—if not most—of the current activities of multinational corporations, but also many of the *non*economic links between "developed" nations and the Third World; no matter how well-intentioned, these often end up being unequal or exploitative owing to the enormous differences in resources on the two sides. This is not to say, of course, that no contacts with the Third World should be initiated, only that there is an obligation on the part of those doing so to ensure that they are established on a basis of equality and reciprocity.

The Crucial Link—The Scholar

If these two courses of action we have outlined—agitation for change in domestic priorities and the building of transnational contacts—do indeed have a chance to enhance the prospects for world peace, then it is a crucial responsibility of the concerned scholar to promote them, not only by advocacy but by example. In professional associations, university bodies, and in countless ways in contacts with the larger community there exist opportunities for scholars to further these goals in the course of performing their duties. Most important of all, perhaps, is the influence they may exert in the classroom; although most university teachers do not, and perhaps should not influence the fundamental values of their students to any significant degree, it is of crucial importance that future elites, mid-elites, and attentive publics be made aware of the urgency of the problem of war and of what has been discovered that might constitute at least a partial solution.

But of course the scholar's fundamental responsibility is for the creation and not merely the dissemination and utilization of knowledge. As has been demonstrated many times in this study, we have barely begun to study those processes and conditions which determine whether or not interaction between and among nations will result in violent conflict. Since, as noted above, preliminary research can be very misleading, the scholar must come to accept even greater professional responsibilities in this area.

There is one last thing. It behooves the scholar not only to generate, disseminate, and act upon knowledge, but in so doing conduct himself in such a way that he creates a *respect* for knowledge in others. For, as Abelard first pointed out, the fact that man has a faculty for ratiocination engenders a corresponding responsibility to use it to best advantage; the scholar's first duty is to perform his work so as to keep this truth constantly before us all.

Appendix

Appendix

Data Sources for the Indices of the Independent Variables

General

ALMANAC DE GOTHA. Gotha: Justus Perthes, 1764-1942.

France. Ministre du Commerce. DOCUMENTS STATISTIQUES SUR LA FRANCE. Paris: De L'imprimerie Royale, 1835.

_____. Statistique Generale. ANNUAIRE STATISTIQUE. Paris: Imprimerie National, 1878.

Germany. Statistisches Reichsamt. STATISTISCHES JAHRBUCH FUR DAS DEUTSCHE REICH. Berlin: Hobbing, 1880-.

Great Britain. Board of Trade. STATISTICAL ABSTRACT FOR THE PRINCIPAL AND OTHER FOREIGN COUNTRIES. . . . London: H. Maj. Stat. Off., 1874-1914.

League of Nations. ANNUAIRE STATISTIQUE DE LA SOCIETE DES NATIONS. Geneva, 1927-42.

Mitchell, B.R. ABSTRACT OF BRITISH HISTORICAL STATISTICS. London: Cambridge University Press, 1962.

Mulhall, Michael G. DICTIONARY OF STATISTICS. 4th Rev. Ed. London: Routledge, 1899.

STATESMAN'S YEARBOOK. London: Macmillan, 1864-.

Sweden. Statistiska Centralbyran. HISTORISK STATISK FOR SVERIGE. 3 Vols. Stockholm: Statens Reproduktionsanstalt, 1955, 1959, 1960.

United Nations. STATISTICAL YEARBOOK. New York, 1948-.

United States. Bureau of the Census. HISTORICAL STATISTICS OF THE UNITED STATES, 1789-1945. Washington: Gov't. Printing Off., 1960.

Webb, Augustus D. NEW DICTIONARY OF STATISTICS. London: Routledge, 1911.

Woytinsky, Vladimer S. DIE WELT IN ZAHLEN. 7 Bd. Berlin: Rudolf Mosse, 1925-28.

_____. WORLD COMMERCE AND GOVERNMENT. New York: Twentieth Century Fund, 1955.

_____. WORLD POPULATION AND PRODUCTION. New York: Twentieth Century Fund, 1953.

Demographic

Durand, John. "The Population Statistics of China, A.D. 2-1953," POPULATION STUDIES, Vol. 13, No. 3 (March, 1960).

Eason, W.W. "The Soviet Population Today," FOREIGN AFFAIRS. XXXVII. (July, 1959.)

United Nations. Statistical Office. Department of Economic and Social Affairs. DEMOGRAPHIC YEARBOOK. New York, 1960.

Weber, Adna Ferrin. THE GROWTH OF CITIES IN THE NINETEENTH CENTURY. A STUDY IN STATISTICS. Ithaca, New York: Cornell University Press, 1963.

Military

Belgium. Ministre des Finances. Chambre des Representants. COMPTE RENDU DES RECETTES ET DEPENSES DU ROYAUME PENDANT L'ANNEE 1838. Bruxelles: M. Hayez, Imprimeur de L'academie royale, 1840.

Belgium. Ministere des Finances. Chambre des Representants. STATISTIQUE GENERALE DES RECETTES ET DES DEPENSES DU ROYAUME DE BELGIQUE 1840-85. Bruxelles: M. Hayez, Imprimeur de l'academie royale de Belgique, 1889.

Bogart, Ernest L. DIRECT AND INDIRECT COSTS OF THE GREAT WORLD WAR. Carnegie Endowment for International Peace. New York: Oxford University Press, 1919.

Curtiss, John Shelton. THE RUSSIAN ARMY UNDER NICHOLAS I. 1825-1855. Durham, N.C.: Duke University Press, 1965.

Erickson, John. THE SOVIET HIGH COMMAND (1918-41). New York: St. Martin's Press, 1962.

ZUR FINANZIELLEN SEITE DER MILITAIRFRAGE. Berlin: Verlag der Königlichen Geheimen Ober-Hofbuchdruckerei, 1862. (Pamphlet in the Parson's Library Collection. Pamphlets—Finance, 4. University of Michigan Library.)

France. Ministere des Finances. PROPOSITIONS DE LOIS RELATIVES A L'OUVERTURE DE CREDITS EXTRAORDINAIRES POUR LE SERVICE DE 1823 ET A LA FIXATION DU BUGDET DES DEPENSES ET DES RECETTES DE 1824. Paris: Imprimerie Royale, 1823.

_____. COMPTE GENERAL DE L'ADMINISTRATIONS DES FINANCES RENDU POUR L'ANNEE 1837. Paris: De L'imprimerie Royale, 1838.

Howard, Michael, THE FRANCO PRUSSIAN WAR. New York: Macmillan, 1962.

League of Nations. ARMAMENTS YEARBOOK. Geneva, 1926-40/41.

Liu, F.F. A MILITARY HISTORY OF MODERN CHINA, 1924-1949. Princeton: Princeton University Press, 1956.

Malchus, C.A. Freiherrn von. HANDBUCH DER FINANZWISSENSCHAFT UND FINANZVERWALTUNG. Stuttgart and Tubingen: J.G. Cotta' schen Buchhandlung, 1830.

Klein, Burton H. GERMANY'S ECONOMIC PREPARATIONS FOR WAR. Cambridge: Harvard University Press, 1959.

Powell, Ralph L. THE RISE OF CHINESE MILITARY POWER, 1895-1912. Princeton: Princeton University Press, 1959.

Prussia. Statistisches Landesamt. TABELLEN UND AMTLICHE NACHRICH-TEN UBER DEN PREUSSISCHEN STAAT FUR DAS JAHR 1849. IV. Berlin: A.W. Hayn, 1853.

Quetelet, Adolphe J. RECHERCHES STATISTIQUES SUR LE ROXAUME DES PAYS-BAS. Bruxelles: Chez. H. Tarlier, 1829.

Industrial

American Iron and Steel Assoc. STATISTICS OF THE AMERICAN AND FOREIGN IRON TRADES. 1868, 1871-1911.

British Iron and Steel Federation. STATISTICAL YEARBOOK. London, 1951.

Burnham, Thomas H. IRON AND STEEL IN BRITAIN, 1870-1930. London: G. Allen Unwin, 1943.

Ehlers, Joseph H. THE PRODUCTION OF IRON AND STEEL IN JAPAN. Washington: Gov't. Printing Off., 1929.

Great Britain. Directorate of Overseas Geological Surveys. STATISTICAL SUMMARY OF THE MINERAL INDUSTRY. London: H.M.S.O., 1920-.

Putnam, Palmer C. ENERGY IN THE FUTURE. New York: D. Van Nostrand, 1953.

Smith, Harry B.A. STATISTICAL RECORD OF THE BRITISH IRON AND STEEL INDUSTRY. Washington: Gov't. Printing Off., 1922.

United Nations. Statistical Papers. Series J. No. 1. WORLD ENERGY SUPPLIES IN SELECTED YEARS, 1929-1950. New York: Statistical Office of the United Nations. Department of Economic Affairs, 1952.

World Power Conferences. STATISTICAL YEARBOOK OF WORLD POWER CONFERENCES. No. 1-9. 1933/34-1954-57. London: The Central Office, World Power Conference, 1936-60.

Bibliography

Bibliography

Adams, J. Stacey, "Wage Inequities, Productivity, and Work Quality," INDUS-
TRIAL RELATIONS, v. 3 (1963), pp. 9-16.

_____. "Inequity in Social Exchange," in Leonard Berkowitz (ed.), AD-
VANCES IN EXPERIMENTAL SOCIAL PSYCHOLOGY, v. 2, N.Y.: Academic Press, 1965, pp. 267-99.

Adams, Stuart, "Status Congruency as a Variable in Small Group Performance,"
SOCIAL FORCES, v. 32, no. 1 (Oct. 1953), pp. 16-22.

Alker, Hayward R., Jr., STATISTICS AND POLITICS: THE NEED FOR
CAUSAL DATA ANALYSIS, Ann Arbor, Mich., unpublished manuscript,
1966.

Almanach de Gotha, Gotha, Justus Perthes, 1764-1942.

Benoit-Smullyan, E., "Status, Status Types, and Status Interrelationships,"
AMERICAN SOCIOLOGICAL REVIEW, v. 9, (1944), pp. 151-61.

Berelson, Bernard, Paul Lazarsfeld, and William McPhee, VOTING, Chicago:
University of Chicago Press, 1954.

Blakeslee, George H., "The Japanese Monroe Doctrine," FOREIGN AFFAIRS,
v. 11, no. 4 (July 1933), pp. 671-81.

Blalock, Hubert, CAUSAL INFERENCES IN NON-EXPERIMENTAL RE-
SEARCH, Chapel Hill: University of North Carolina Press, 1962.

_____. "The Identification Problem and Theory Building: The Case of Status
Inconsistency," AMERICAN SOCIOLOGICAL REVIEW, v. 31 (1966), pp.
52-63.

_____. "Status Inconsistency, Social Mobility, and Structural Effects,"
AMERICAN SOCIOLOGICAL REVIEW, v. 32 (1967), pp. 790-801.

_____. "Status Inconsistency and Interaction: Some Alternative Models,"
AMERICAN JOURNAL OF SOCIOLOGY, v. 73 (1967), pp. 305-15.

Boudon, Raymond, "A New Look at Correlational Analysis," in Hubert M.
Blalock and Ann B. Blalock, METHODOLOGY IN SOCIAL RESEARCH,
N.Y.: McGraw-Hill, 1968, pp. 199-235.

Boulding, Kenneth E., CONFLICT AND DEFENSE: A GENERAL THEORY,
N.Y.: Harper and Row, 1962.

Campbell, Angus et al., THE AMERICAN VOTER, N.Y.: Wiley and Sons, 1960.

Caplan, Nathan G. and Jeffery M. Paige, "A Study of Ghetto Rioters,"
SCIENTIFIC AMERICAN, v. 219, no. 2 (August 1968), pp. 15-21.

Cassell, Ronald, POWER-BASE CODING RULES, Ann Arbor, Mich., unpublished manuscript, 1966.

Choucri, Nazli and Robert C. North, "The Determinants of International
Violence," PEACE RESEARCH SOCIETY PAPERS, v. 12 (1969), pp. 33-63.

Christ, Carl F., ECONOMETRIC MODELS AND METHODS, N.Y.: Wiley and
Sons, 1966.

Clark, J.V., A PRELIMINARY INVESTIGATION OF SOME UNCONSCIOUS ASSUMPTIONS AFFECTING LABOR EFFICIENCY IN EIGHT SUPER-MARKETS, unpublished doctoral dissertation, Harvard University, 1958.

Claude, Inis L., POWER AND INTERNATIONAL RELATIONS, N.Y.: Random House, 1962.

_____ . "The United Nations' Use of Military Force," JOURNAL OF CON-FLICT RESOLUTION, v. 7, no. 2 (1963), pp. 117-29.

_____ . SWORDS INTO PLOUGHSHARES, (4th ed.), N.Y.: Random House, 1971.

Cofer, C.N., and M.H. Appley, MOTIVATION: THEORY AND RESEARCH, N.Y.: Wiley and Sons, 1964.

Coombs, Clyde H., A THEORY OF DATA, N.Y.: Wiley and Sons, 1964.

Deutsch, Karl W., THE ANALYSIS OF INTERNATIONAL RELATIONS, Englewood Cliffs, N.J.: Prentice-Hall, 1968.

Deutsch, Karl W. and Dieter Senghaas, "A Framework for a Theory of War and Peace," in Albert Lepawsky et al. (eds.), THE SEARCH FOR WORLD ORDER, N.Y.: Appleton-Century-Crofts, 1971.

East, Maurice A., STRATIFICATION AND INTERNATIONAL POLITICS: AN EMPIRICAL STUDY EMPLOYING THE INTERNATIONAL SYSTEMS APPROACH, unpublished doctoral dissertation, Princeton University, 1969.

Eckstein, Harry, DIVISION AND COHESION IN DEMOCRACY: A STUDY OF NORWAY, Princeton, N.J.: Princeton University Press, 1966.

ENCYCLOPAEDIA BRITANNICA, Edinburgh: Bell and McFarquhar, 1771.

Fenchel, G.H., J.H. Monderer, and E.L. Hartley, "Subjective Status and the Equilibration Hypothesis," JOURNAL OF ABNORMAL AND SOCIAL PSYCHOLOGY, v. 25 (1951), pp. 476-9.

Forbes, Hugh Donald and Edward R. Tufte, "A Note of Caution in Causal Modelling," AMERICAN POLITICAL SCIENCE REVIEW, v. 62, no. 4 (Dec. 1968), pp. 1258-64.

Fossum, Egil, "Factors Influencing the Occurrence of Military Coups d'Etat in Latin America," JOURNAL OF PEACE RESEARCH, no. 3 (1967), pp. 228-51.

Fucks, Wilhelm, FORMELN ZUR MACHT: PROGNOSEN UBER VOLKER, WIRTSCHAFT, POTENTIALE, Stuttgart: Deutsch Verlagsanfalt, 1965.

Galtung, Johan, "Rank and Social Integration: A Multidimensional Approach," in Joseph Berger, Morris Zelditch, and Bo Anderson, (eds.), SOCIOLOGICAL THEORIES IN PROGRESS, Boston: Houghton Mifflin, 1966, pp. 145-98.

Galtung, Johan, "A Structural Theory of Aggression," JOURNAL OF PEACE RESEARCH, no. 2 (1964), pp. 95-119.

Galtung, Johan, "Reply to Gudmund Hernes," JOURNAL OF PEACE RE-SEARCH, no. 1 (1969), pp. 75-6.

German, F. Clifford, "A Tentative Evaluation of World Power," JOURNAL OF CONFLICT RESOLUTION, v. 4, no. 1 (1960), pp. 138-44.

Goffman, I.W., "Status Inconsistency and Preference for Change in the the Power Distribution," AMERICAN SOCIOLOGICAL REVIEW, v. 22 (1957), pp. 275-81.

Greenstein, Fred I., "The Impact of Personality on Politics: An Attempt to Clear Away Underbrush," AMERICAN POLITICAL SCIENCE REVIEW, v. 61, no. 2 (Sept. 1967), pp. 629-41.

Gulick, Edward V., EUROPE'S CLASSICAL BALANCE OF POWER, Ithaca, N.Y.: Cornell University Press, 1955.

Haas, Ernst, BEYOND THE NATION STATE, Stanford: Stanford University Press, 1964.

Hernes, Gudmund, "On Rank Disequilibrium and Coups d'Etat," JOURNAL OF PEACE RESEARCH, no. 1 (1969), pp. 65-72.

Herz, John H., INTERNATIONAL POLITICS IN THE ATOMIC AGE, N.Y.: Columbia University Press, 1959.

Hirschman, Albert O., NATIONAL POWER AND THE STRUCTURE OF FOREIGN TRADE, Los Angeles: University of California Press, 1969.

Hobbes, Thomas, THE LEVIATHAN, edited with an introduction by Michael Oakeshott, Oxford: Basil Blackwell, 1955.

Hobson, John, IMPERIALISM (3rd edition), London: Allen and Unwin, 1938.

Hoffman, Stanley, THE THEORY OF INTERNATIONAL RELATIONS, Englewood Cliffs, N.J.: Prentice-Hall, Inc., 1960.

Hyman, Martin D., "Determining the Effects of Status Inconsistency," PUBLIC OPINION QUARTERLY, v. 30, no. 1 (Spring 1966), pp. 120-29.

Ingham, Kenneth, THE MAKING OF MODERN UGANDA, London: Allen and Unwin, 1957.

Jackson, E.F., "Status Consistency and Symptoms of Stress," AMERICAN SOCIOLOGICAL REVIEW, v. 27 (1962), pp. 336-43.

Johnston, J., ECONOMETRIC METHODS, N.Y.: McGraw-Hill, 1963.

Kaplan, Morton A., SYSTEM AND PROCESS IN INTERNATIONAL POLITICS, N.Y.: Wiley and Sons, 1957.

Kelly, K. Dennis and William J. Chambliss, "Status Consistency and Political Attitudes," AMERICAN SOCIOLOGICAL REVIEW, v. 31 (1966), pp. 375-81.

Kelman, Herbert C. (ed.), INTERNATIONAL BEHAVIOR: A SOCIAL-PSYCHOLOGICAL ANALYSIS, N.Y.: Holt, Rinehart, and Winston, 1965.

Kenkel, W.F., "The Relationship between Status Consistency and Politico-Economic Attitudes," AMERICAN SOCIOLOGICAL REVIEW, v. 21 (1956), pp. 365-8.

Kimberley, James C., "A Theory of Status Equilibration," in Joseph Berger, Morris Zelditch, and Bo Anderson (eds.), SOCIOLOGICAL THEORIES IN PROGRESS, Boston: Houghton Mifflin, 1966, pp. 213-26.

Kuznets, Simon, MODERN ECONOMIC GROWTH, New Haven, Conn.: Yale University Press, 1966.

Lagos, Gustavo, INTERNATIONAL STRATIFICATION AND THE UNDER-DEVELOPED COUNTRIES, Chapel Hill: University of North Carolina Press, 1963.

Lenski, Gerhard, "Status Crystallization: A Non-vertical Dimension of Social Status," AMERICAN SOCIOLOGICAL REVIEW, v. 19 (1954), pp. 405-13.

_____. "Social Participation and Status Crystallization," AMERICAN SOCIOLOGICAL REVIEW, v. 21 (1956), pp. 458-64.

_____. POWER AND PRIVILEGE, N.Y.: McGraw-Hill, 1966.

_____. "Status Inconsistency and the Vote: A Four Nation Test," AMERICAN SOCIOLOGICAL REVIEW, v. 32 (1967), pp. 298-301.

Lipset, Seymour Martin, POLITICAL MAN, N.Y.: Doubleday, 1959.

Masters, Roger D., "World Politics as a Primitive Political System," WORLD POLITICS, v. 16, no. 4 (July 1964), pp. 595-619.

Midlarsky, Manus and Raymond Tanter, "Toward a Theory of Political Instability in Latin America," JOURNAL OF PEACE RESEARCH, no. 3 (1967), pp. 209-27.

_____. STATUS INCONSISTENCY AND THE ONSET OF INTERNATIONAL WARFARE, unpublished Ph.D. dissertation, Northwestern University, 1968.

Mitrany, David, A WORKING PEACE SYSTEM (4th ed.), Oxford: Oxford University Press, 1946.

Morgenstern, Oskar, ON THE ACCURACY OF ECONOMIC OBSERVATIONS, (2nd edition), Princeton, N.J.: Princeton University Press, 1963.

Morgenthau, Hans J., POLITICS AMONG NATIONS (4th edition), N.Y.: A.A. Knopf, 1967.

Nicholas, H.G., THE UNITED NATIONS AS A POLITICAL INSTITUTION (2nd edition), N.Y.: Oxford University Press, 1963.

Organski, A.F.K., WORLD POLITICS (2nd edition), N.Y.: A.A. Knopf, 1968.

Rae, D.W. and M. Taylor, THE ANALYSIS OF POLITICAL CLEAVAGES, New Haven: Yale University Press, 1970.

Robinson, W.S., "Ecological Correlations and the Behavior of Individuals," AMERICAN SOCIOLOGICAL REVIEW, v. 15 (1950), pp. 351-7.

Rosecrance, Richard N., ACTION AND REACTION IN WORLD POLITICS, Boston: Little, Brown and Co., 1963.

Rosenau, James N., "Private Preferences and Political Responsibilities: The Relative Potency of Individual and Role Variables in the Behavior of U.S. Senators," in J. David Singer (ed.), QUANTITATIVE INTERNATIONAL POLITICS: INSIGHTS AND EVIDENCE, N.Y.: Free Press, 1968.

Ross, Edward Alsworth, THE PRINCIPLES OF SOCIOLOGY, N.Y.: The Century Co., 1920.

Russett, Bruce M. et al., WORLD HANDBOOK OF POLITICAL INDICATORS, New Haven: Yale University Press, 1958.

_____. INTERNATIONAL REGIONS AND THE INTERNATIONAL SYSTEM, Chicago: Rand McNally, 1967.

_____ . "Components of an Operational Theory of Alliance Formation," JOURNAL OF CONFLICT RESOLUTION, v. 12, no. 3 (1968), pp. 285-301.

Sayles, L.R., BEHAVIOR OF INDUSTRIAL WORK GROUPS: PREDICTION AND CONTROL, N.Y.: Wiley and Sons, 1958.

Segal, David R., "Status Inconsistency, Cross-Pressures, and American Political Behavior, AMERICAN SOCIOLOGICAL REVIEW, v. 33 (1968), pp. 352-9.

Shils, Edward, "The Intellectuals in the Political Development of the New States," WORLD POLITICS, v. 12, no. 3 (April 1960), pp. 329-68.

Siegal, Sidney, NON-PARAMETRIC STATISTICS FOR THE BEHAVIORAL SCIENCES, N.Y.: McGraw-Hill, 1956.

Singer, J. David, "Threat Perception and the Armament-Tension Dilemma," JOURNAL OF CONFLICT RESOLUTION, v. 2, no. 1 (1958), pp. 90-105.

_____ . "Inter Nation Influence: A Formal Model," AMERICAN POLITICAL SCIENCE REVIEW, v. 57, no. 2 (June 1963), pp. 420-30.

Singer, J. David and Paul Ray, "Decision-Making in Conflict: From Inter-Personal to Inter-National Relations, BULLETIN OF THE MENNINGER CLINIC, v. 30, no. 5 (Sept. 1966), pp. 300-12.

Singer, J. David and Melvin Small, "The Composition and Status Ordering of the International System," WORLD POLITICS, v. 18, no. 2 (Jan. 1966), pp. 236-82.

_____ . "Alliance Aggregation and the Onset of War, 1815-1945," in J. David Singer (ed.), QUANTITATIVE INTERNATIONAL POLITICS: INSIGHTS AND EVIDENCE, N.Y.: The Free Press, 1968.

_____ . THE WAGES OF WAR: A STATISTICAL HANDBOOK, 1816-1965, N.Y.: Wiley and Sons, 1972.

_____ . "The Diplomatic Importance of States, 1816-1965: An Extension of the Basic Data," Ann Arbor: Mental Health Research Institute preprint, 1970.

Singer, J. David and Michael D. Wallace, "Inter-Governmental Organization and the Preservation of Peace, 1816-1965: Some Bivariate Relationships," INTERNATIONAL ORGANIZATION, v. 24, no. 3 (Summer 1970), pp. 520-47.

STATESMAN'S YEARBOOK, London: Macmillan, 1864.

Tuchman, Barbara, THE GUNS OF AUGUST, N.Y.: Macmillan, 1962.

Tufte, Edward, "Improving Data Analysis in Political Science," WORLD POLITICS, v. 21, no. 4 (July 1969), pp. 641-54.

Turner, Malcolm E. and Charles D. Stevens, "Regression Analysis of Causal Paths," BIOMETRICS, v. 15, no. 2 (1959), pp. 236-58.

United Nations, DEMOGRAPHIC YEARBOOK, N.Y.: Statistical Office, Department of Economic and Social Affairs, 1948.

_____ . STATISTICAL YEARBOOK, N.Y.: Statistical Office, Department of Economic and Social Affairs, 1948-.

Wallace, Michael D. and J. David Singer, "Inter-Governmental Organization in the Global System, 1816-1964: A Quantitative Description," INTERNATIONAL ORGANIZATION, v. 29, no. 2 (Spring 1970), pp. 239-87.

Wallace, Michael D., "Power, Status, and International War, 1820-1964," JOURNAL OF PEACE RESEARCH, 1971, no. 1, pp. 23-35.

_____ , "The Radical Critique of Peace Research: An Exposition and Interpretation," PEACE RESEARCH REVIEWS, v. 4, no. 4, pp. 24-51.

_____ , "Status, Formal Organization, and Arms Races as Factors Leading to the Onset of International War, 1820-1964," in Bruce M. Russett (ed.), PEACE, WAR, AND NUMBERS, San Francisco: Sage Press, 1972, pp. 49-69.

_____ , "Alliance Polarization, Cross-Cutting, and International War, 1815-1964: A Measurement Procedure and Some Preliminary Evidence," JOURNAL OF CONFLICT RESOLUTION, v. 17, no. 3, (September. 1973), forthcoming.

Waltz, Kenneth H., MAN, THE STATE, AND WAR, N.Y.: Columbia University Press, 1959.

Waltz, Kenneth N., "International Structure, National Force, and the Balance of World Power," in James N. Rosenau (ed.), INTERNATIONAL POLITICS AND FOREIGN POLICY (2nd edition), N.Y.: Free Press, 1969, pp. 304-14.

Weber, Max, "Class, Status, and Party," in Reinhard Bendix and Seymour Martin Lipset (eds.), CLASS, STATUS, AND POWER, Glencoe, Ill.: Free Press, 1953, pp. 63-75.

Weiner, Myron, THE POLITICS OF SCARCITY, Chicago: University of Chicago Press, 1962.

Wesolowski, Wlodzimierz, "Some Notes on the Functional Theory of Stratification," in Reinhard Bendix and Seymour Martin Lipset (eds.), CLASS, STATUS, AND POWER (2nd edition), N.Y.: Free Press, 1966, pp. 64-8.

Wilkenfeld, Jonathan, "Domestic and Foreign Conflict Behavior of Nations," JOURNAL OF PEACE RESEARCH, no. 1 (1968), pp. 56-69.

Wright, Sewell, "The Method of Path Coefficients," ANNALS OF MATHEMATICAL STATISTICS, v. 5 (1934), pp. 161-215.

Wright, Quincy, A STUDY OF WAR, Chicago: University of Chicago Press, 1965.

Zetterberg, Hans L., "On Motivation," in Joseph Berger, Morris Zelditch, and Bo Anderson (eds.), SOCIOLOGICAL THEORIES IN PROGRESS, Boston: Houghton Mifflin, 1966, pp. 124-41.

About the Author

Michael D. Wallace was born in Montreal and obtained the Master's Degree at McGill University. He obtained his doctorate at the University of Michigan in 1970, and is closely associated with the Correlates of War Project based at the Mental Health Research Institute in Ann Arbor.

He is a contributor to several peace research journals, and has held offices in the International Peace Science Society and the Canadian Peace Research and Education Association. At present he teaches political science at the University of British Columbia, where he is a member of the Governing Council of the Institute of International Relations. He lives in Vancouver with his wife, Eileen, their son, Ian, and such other companions as they invent from time to time.